INDIAN INDUSTRIALISATION

TRAJECTORY REDEFINED

Bestseller by the same author:
Management by Walking

INDIAN INDUSTRIALISATION

TRAJECTORY REDEFINED

Outcome of Prime Minister Modi's strategic visits
to diverse parts of the globe

Dr. AK AGARWAL

ATLANTIC
PUBLISHERS & DISTRIBUTORS (P) LTD

First published in India in 2016 by
Atlantic Publishers & Distributors (P) Ltd., India

PB: ISBN 978-81-269-2132-4
HB: ISBN 978-81-269-2133-1

Published by
ATLANTIC
PUBLISHERS & DISTRIBUTORS (P) LTD
7/22, Ansari Road, Darya Ganj, New Delhi-110002, India
Phones : +91-11-40775252, 23273880, 23275880, 23280451
Fax: +91-11-23285873
Web: www.atlanticbooks.com
E-mail: orders@atlanticbooks.com

Branch Office
5, Nallathambi Street, Wallajah Road, Chennai-600002, India
Phones : +91-44-64611085, 32413319
E-mail: chennai@atlanticbooks.com

Typeset in 11/14 Electra LT Regular

Printed and bound at
Nice Printing Press, A-33/3A, Site-IV, Industrial Area,
Sahibabad, Ghaziabad, U.P., India

CONTENTS

Contents

PREFACE

"Sound strategy starts with having the right goal."
–**Michael Porter**, Professor, Harvard Business School

Today, globalisation is opening many doors for countries, irrespective of whether these are emerging countries or developed ones. According to Eduardo Paes, a Brazilian author, *"Globalisation has produced a new level of interdependence among us. Economic integration is the first strong evidence of a new era."*

India is equipped with big bank of factors in its favour – intellectual power, research bent of mind, vibrant and deep-rooted democracy, rich culture and heritage, high degree of religious tolerance, peace loving and patriotic population, internationally recognised legal/ accounting systems, rich natural resources, self-reliant agriculture and many more. From this, it is quite evident that India just cannot be ignored in the world scenario, not only in terms of its area and population, but also in terms of its economic prowess. On the state of the global economy, Christine Lagarde, Managing Director, IMF, has this to say, *"Among emerging economies, if there is any growth that is in India. India is among the few bright spots in the global economy."*

Add to this the intellectual resource 'drained' out of India that fuels the industries and technologies of the developed world today and there is no doubt that India remains the promised fertile land of opportunities that are yet to be encashed. India is now notching up to assert itself on the world stage and the storm created by Prime Minister Modi by forging long-term strategic relationship with the leaders of the world, during his foreign visits, is bound to have positive consequences.

It is a well proven fact that face-to-face interaction is by far the most result-oriented option, than exchanging official mail via electronic and other media. American writer, Felicia Day was not off the mark when she said, "*Social media is an amazing tool, but it's really the face-to-face interaction that makes a long-term impact.*"

India has been a key contributor to Paris agreement on climate change because of healthy relationships created with most of the countries in the world, as a reflection of strategic visits by PM Modi. The outcome was visible in Paris Summit for Climate Change Agreement. India's voice was not only heard and welcomed, but was also included to a large extent. Climate change convention in Paris throws up a different challenge as well as opportunities to the industries in India, as well as to climate change scientists.

The international wave generated by Modi has not only brought India into the world's notice, but has also given a new roadmap to the country's industrialisation. The world's attention is getting focussed on India and is goading the country to build its infrastructure to meet the new demands. This initiative has certainly woken up India from its sloth.

Programmes that have far-reaching effects are already making waves, such as 'Make in India', 'Skill India', 'Start up India',

'Digital India', and others. This has all the makings of giving India self-reliance.

From time immemorial, India and Korea enjoyed a deep-rooted relationship in the fields of culture, history, trade, industry and diplomacy. While India is bigger in size, population and, more importantly, cultural diversity, Korea is much advanced in industrial development. The model of industrialisation followed by Korea can be a good benchmark to implement, particularly in India where, like in Korea, spiritualism is more valued than materialism. In addition, combination of large conglomerates called Chaebols and strong bank of SMEs have been the backbone of growth in the Korean economy. There are thus huge opportunities for cooperation between the two countries if India effectively utilises Korean firms as partners in its process of industrialisation. Strong and competitive SMEs would promise economic prosperity in the largest democracy on the planet. This is important for true globalisation and world peace.

The book authored by Dr. AK Agarwal, who has also written a previous bestseller *Management by Walking*, is a brilliant take on the trajectory being redefined in the industrial sector in the wake of Modi's foreign initiatives. Written in simple language, the book makes for stimulating reading for all. The book presents deep insights of the future shaping of industrialisation in India, which makes it a remarkable tool for business leaders across the globe to sharpen their strategies, while doing business in this great country – India.

In the concluding chapter, *On the Home Turf – The Road Ahead*, the author presents the improvements that are needed in India to make Modi's initiatives a success. More so, since these initiatives have made India a global magnet that is attracting a host of developed and developing countries. It is time that collectively all citizens of India understand the new ground realities without losing any more time.

It is pertinent to put forth here the arguments of Henry Ford, Founder of the Ford Motor Company, who says, "*If there is any one secret of success, it lies in the ability to get the other person's point of view and see things from that person's angle as well as from your own.*"

Prof. Choelsoon Park

Professor, Seoul National University, Korea,
Former Chairman, Board of Directors, Sinhan Bank, Korea,
Member, Editorial Board, Long Range Planning (Elsevier)
& Faculty, London Business School, UK

ACKNOWLEDGEMENTS

The current growth trajectory of Indian industrialisation is witnessing an exceptional height. This could be attributed to the international, business-based, endeavours of Hon'ble Prime Minister, Shri Narendra Modi, in particular and the Union Government, in general. Being an engineer myself, I have had a ringside view of the recent happenings on the industrialisation front and this has inspired me to write this book.

During his numerous foreign visits, Modi brainstormed on the prominent issues which according to him are prerequisite for the bright future of industry in India. His efforts to garner support of top technology holders, innovators, influencers, entrepreneurs and social activists through his interaction at international level are unparalleled and remain absolutely essential for success in today's fast changing globalised scenario.

There is hardly any doubt that the Indian industry needs to rebase itself in order to grow and reap the fruits of strategic understanding reached during foreign visits of PM Modi. Yasuhiro Sato is right in stating, "*Clearly differentiated strategy is the key to growth.*" PM Modi's foreign initiatives have woken the Indian industries to this new realisation.

My father late Mr. CL Agarwal and my mother late Mrs. Saveti Devi have remained a motivating factor for me in my academic pursuit and are an inspiration for this book too that envisages shedding light on the transformation taking place in Indian industrialisation through the tireless efforts of our beloved Prime Minister.

I convey my sincere thanks to Prof. Choelsoon Park, Professor, Seoul National University, Korea and Member, Editorial Board, Long Range Planning (Elsevier) for penning the Preface and Dr. Sushil, Professor, Management Studies, Indian Institute of Technology, Delhi, for his valuable ideas and suggestions in bringing out the book.

My gratitude also extends to the distinguished management experts, Mr. Jean-Marie Vanalderweireldt of Belgium and Dr. Tony Michell of United Kingdom for providing niche international perspective on Indian industrialisation. It is important to mention that Mr. KG Suresh, Senior Consulting Editor, Doordarshan News, Govt. of India, has been indispensable while sharing his ideas on the state of industries in the country.

I express my immense appreciation to Padma Shri Shri Brahmdev Sharma (Bhaiji) for his unstinted support in providing valuable recommendations, particularly the inclusion of the role of general masses that play an indispensable part in the Indian industrialisation.

I feel indebted to Mr. Pradeep Kashyap, Mr. Ranjan Kumar Singh and Mr. Arvind Mathur, noted intellectuals in print and audio-visual media, who have been of immense help with their invaluable inputs in putting together this book. I also acknowledge the contribution of Press Information Bureau (PIB), Government of India, for enriching the book with photographs of PM Modi's visit to various countries. I especially thank Mr. Nirmalya Datta, who has extended full support in meticulously checking the text and providing valuable suggestions.

I also acknowledge the commendable efforts put in by the staff of Atlantic Publishers & Distributors (P) Ltd. for their speedy and quality production. I would particularly like to thank Mr. Manish Gupta, its Managing Director for his whole-hearted support all throughout.

I am deeply indebted to my wife, Neera, for her encouragement, wise counsel, endless support and much more. I am grateful to my son, Ankur, and daughter-in-law, Sonam, who have extraordinarily facilitated the activities with passion and dedication. I am also very much appreciative of my daughter, Nikita, for her diligent and attentive contribution in the overall layout of the book.

While due care has been taken to put forth the data, information, suggestions and ideas, there are possibilities of inadvertent errors despite our best efforts. Errors, if any, will be corrected in the next edition after getting valuable feedback from the respected readers.

I firmly believe that nothing can materialise without the grace of God, the Almighty; and thus I consider myself blessed that I could accomplish this task. To me He has been a constant guiding force; and to Him, I bow in reverence.

Dr. AK Agarwal

INTRODUCTION

In this era of globalisation, no country can ever progress in isolation as PM Modi firmly believes, "*No country can exist on its own, we have to take other countries along.*"

Indeed, robust foundation for industrialisation coupled with faster growth of economy through globalisation becomes the key to success for development. It is imperative to ensure that development is truly inclusive and is not confined to a few segments of the society. Each and every citizen – whether rich or poor, rural or urban, industrialist or farmer, educated or uneducated, of any cast or creed – has to be a stakeholder in the path of progress.

It is unfortunate to note that despite adequate resources and manpower, India's index remains very poor with low per capita income as compared to smaller counties. Very often, excuses for this tardy progress are attributed to rampant corruption and to the unchecked population growth. But more importantly, it is also a poor reflection on how we have managed our resources during these past years. There had been no check on brain-drain. People went abroad for lack of opportunities in the country. Scientists from India manage NASA (National Aeronautics and Space Administration) in the US, but fail to see tsunami and other natural disasters in their own country.

Probably in a bid to win back its draining brain, the Prime Minister is going places and meeting the Indian diaspora. Do such organised visits create an impact? Yes, of course. It must be realised that even in this fast track communication age, e-mails cannot replace face-to-face meetings. In the words of Mina Chang (2015) "*Managing a successful team – and, consequently, a successful business – requires personal connections. Business is, in large part, about building relationships.*" It is ultimately the human relationship that leads to successful business. There had been hardly any mention of India in the foreign media. Now the country feels proud that not a day passes when it is not mentioned in the foreign media. Credit for this would certainly go to Prime Minister Narendra Modi, who has visited more than 25 countries in the first year of assuming charge and has managed to establish personal rapport with the world leaders and business houses of several countries. As a result, there has been a quantum jump in FDI (Foreign Direct Investment) in India.

Narendra Modi, as the Chief Minister of Gujarat (2001-2014), had been praised for taking the state to higher development trajectory with speedy industrialisation. But now, as the Prime Minister of India, he is being criticised for paying frequent visits to diverse parts of the globe.

Dan McCrum (2015) has rightly said, "*Sometimes it requires a very long-term perspective to come to a view about what will happen in the near future.*" Whereas now all countries look upon India as a fast emerging economic power and show eagerness to invest in India, the fact of the matter is that the change in the global perspective pertaining to India can be attributed to Modi's initiatives and policies aimed at creating India as an investment hub by assuring a congenial atmosphere for investment, easing visa restrictions and removing other barriers.

Daniel P Myers (2014) remarked that India has long-term growth potential. Axel C Heitmann (2014) too welcomes "*India's recent economic reforms as steps in the right direction*" and states, "*I have no doubt that future reform will strengthen trade and investment ties as well as benefit India's domestic industry.*"

The notable achievements of Modi's regime include the agreement on boundary dispute between India and Bangladesh, which will definitely lead to the promotion of trade and development of small and medium enterprises, thus providing employment to thousands of people. In another instance, Modi conveyed to France that India would buy thirty-six multirole combat aircraft *Rafale*, as early as possible. The agreement contains a clause of 'industry offset', which means ancillary parts of the aircraft would be produced indigenously in due course. This is also aimed at not only saving foreign exchange, but also generating more employment for the Indian youth.

Modi has demonstrated his proactive foreign policy to realise his 'inclusive' development agenda through peace and tranquillity by improving relations with the immediate neighbourhood first, then with the extended neighbourhood (South East Asian Region) and ultimately with the Developed Nations. He has gone an extra mile to improve relations with China, keeping aside the boundary issues; and also with Pakistan with which India had been maintaining a distance, after its complacency in the 26/11 Mumbai terrorist attack. This will not only ensure development of the region, but also create an opportunity for all South Asian countries for investment. In other words, it would generate more employment, leading to the creation of more institutions to train manpower.

Modi surprised all with his diplomatic prowess when he invited SAARC (South Asian Association for Regional Cooperation) leaders to his Swearing-in Ceremony, thus showing his utmost regard for the region. He perhaps took cue from his predecessor and BJP stalwart Atal Bihari Vajpayee, who had said, "*One can change one's friends, but not neighbours*". Strong and prosperous neighbourhood is a must. Modi has a clear vision that he would not be able to carry forward his development agenda unless there was peace in the South Asian region. Modi's doctrine is simple and straightforward, that is, to focus on immediate neighbouring countries in the South Asia, to strengthen ties with extended neighbours in the South East Asia and to project India as a strong and viable economic power among the developed nations.

His Swearing-in Ceremony was marked with the presence of almost all premieres of SAARC nations that included Nawaz Sharif (Pakistan), Hamid Karzai (Afghanistan), Tshering Tobgay (Bhutan), Naveen Ramgoolam (Mauritius), Abdulla Yameen (Maldives), Sushil Koirala (Nepal) and Mahinda Rajapaksa (Sri Lanka). The Bangladesh Prime Minister Sheikh Hasina could not attend due to her scheduled foreign tour, but sent in her Parliamentary Secretary. Modi took the opportunity in holding separate meetings with all these leaders. By doing so, Modi was able to send a strong message of his 'inclusive' foreign policy.

Modi provided a new vision and a much needed impetus to the country's foreign policy so that India's image soared to a higher trajectory in the world. In pursuance of his development agenda he invited NRIs (Non-Resident Indians) to invest more and more in India and for this he eased the visa facilities. He strongly advocated India's case for a permanent membership in the UN (United Nations) Security Council and sought support from across the globe against trans-border terrorism. With his diplomatic prowess and pro-activism, he has almost encompassed the whole world, putting across his vision of inclusive development and peaceful co-existence, thereby reviving the message contained in the UN preamble.

Modi's visit to the US was historic for more reasons than one. There he was not just accorded a grand reception by the Obama Administration, but was also enthusiastically welcomed by the Indian diaspora. He understands too well that the US is one such superpower, with which good relations can help achieve his goal of speedy industrialisation and transform India into 'a strong economic power'. Commenting on the recent initiatives and activities from both the sides, Dr. Walter Ladwig (2015) writes, "*the prospects of a meaningful expansion of Indo-US relations appear to be better today than at any point in the recent past.*"

His outreach to neighbouring countries, such as China, Bhutan, Nepal, Sri Lanka, Bangladesh, Mauritius; Far-East nations of Japan, South Korea and Myanmar, and his bilateral talks with Australia were aimed at bringing foreign investment into India thereby expanding trade and commerce.

There is a big gap between power generation and demand in India. Availability of power is an important factor for economic and industrial development. Bhutan and Nepal that are situated in the Himalayas have the potential of becoming top hydropower producing countries. While on his visit to Bhutan and Nepal, Modi assured them of all possible help in setting up power projects in these nations. He also convinced them that they could sell their surplus power to India in order to improve their own financial situation.

Modi's visit to Mauritius, strategically located in the Indian Ocean, holds significance from the security point of view. Since India's economic interests are inseparably linked with the Indian Ocean, hence maintaining it as a zone of peace is an important aspect of its foreign policy. Mauritius, with a large population owing its origin to India, is the best insurance for India. Moreover, its importance also lies in the fact that it is one of the regions that originates most of the FDI (Foreign Direct Investment) coming into India, as Mauritius continues to corner more than 44 per cent of the FDI coming into the country.

His trip to Japan as the first major destination was most significant as he took off from where his predecessor Dr. Manmohan Singh had left. Modi successfully scripted and showcased his closeness with Japan and its Prime Minister. The visit had multi-dimensional effect on Indo-Japanese bilateral relations – religious, cultural, economic and security scenario.

The presence of Indian diaspora in most countries has presented Modi a free run to address them in Hindi. His popularity among the Indian origin nationals has had the desired effect, not to forget his famous rally at the Madison Square in the USA (United States of America). His engagements in the UN General Assembly, and the US (United States) were noteworthy in bringing the world leaders to observe the International Yoga Day.

There has been criticism of Modi carrying his capitalist friends during the visits. Hardly any government can hope to ignore them, if enough trade and commerce has to be generated during such visits. It has been a permanent fixture of any entourage irrespective of their political affiliations. Even while Presidents/ Prime Ministers/ Ministers of other countries visited India, they were accompanied by a large entourage comprising of trade and business leaders. In fact, to move around with business leaders on tours targeted at foreign relations is an accepted practice the world over.

In all multilateral forums like the UN, ASEAN (Association of Southeast Asian Nations), BRICS (Brazil, Russia, India, China and South Africa), G-20 (Group of 20) and SAARC (South Asian Association for Regional Cooperation), he effectively promoted India's interest by intelligently replacing India's 'Look East' policy with 'Act East' policy, and inviting ASEAN countries to take part in this 'Act East' initiative. At G-20, he raised the issue of black money and again raised it at BRICS in Fortaleza, Brazil. Meanwhile

India's proposal to launch a New Development Bank in Shanghai was accepted, which will have its first President from India.

Modi's initiatives include the policies of 'Neighbourhood First', 'Act East', and 'Link West', together with the Indian Ocean Outreach and India-Pacific Islands Cooperation programs.

To sum up, the impact of Modi's frequent foreign tours has been immense and unprecedented and has helped India regain its stature, not just as the land of awakening, but as a region for opportunities too. Perhaps this has been possible because of the fact that while Modi keeps himself grounded to the best of Indian values, his vision flies high and looks upwards to modern economic ideas and new technologies.

CHAPTER 1

MODI AND 'NEIGHBOURHOOD FIRST' POLICY

Modi's Visits to Neighbouring Countries

• Bhutan • Nepal • Sri Lanka
• Bangladesh • Myanmar

"One can change one's friends, not neighbours."

—Atal Bihari Vajpayee, India's Former Prime Minister

Even before becoming the Prime Minister of India, Modi had envisioned improving India's ties with its immediate neighbours. Thus, it came as no surprise that, once he took over as Prime Minister, one of the major policy initiatives of his government was to shift the focus back on India's immediate neighbours in South Asia. This is being termed as 'Neighbourhood First' Policy.

From the word go, Modi made his intentions clear by inviting all Heads of State/ Governments of SAARC nations for his Swearing-in Ceremony on May 26, 2014. Not only this, he went ahead and held bilateral talks just on the second day of his being sworn in with each and every Heads of State/ Governments, individually. The media was quick to term it as 'Mini SAARC Summit'. And rightly so, the focus of his talks was more economic in nature, than political, based on SAARC principles.

Just to show his seriousness in making India's ties stronger with immediate neighbours, he even asked the Indian scientists at a launch event at ISRO (Indian Space Research Organisation) to work towards developing a dedicated SAARC satellite for the benefit of people of South Asian countries in various fields, such as tele-medicine, e-learning, and the like. This would be an add-on to the currently operating Indian Technical and Economic Cooperation Programme in the region.

Foreign Policy of a country is a continuous process and any new government generally tows the same line as that of its predecessor. But, the Modi Government brought about a significant change in it by putting a strong emphasis on India's relationship with the neighbouring countries by introducing the 'Neighbourhood First' Policy. This was entirely aimed at establishing peace and tranquillity in the region, to realise his own agenda of inclusive development and provide impetus to India's rapid industrialisation, as well as of the region.

BHUTAN: Modi's First Destination (June 15-16, 2014)

"Like milk and water, India and Bhutan cannot be separated." —**Jigme Dorji Wangchuck,** Third King of Bhutan

Modi chose Bhutan as his first destination after assuming charge. It was described as a 'goodwill visit' at the invitation of Bhutan King Jigme Khesar Namgyel Wangchuck and Bhutanese Prime Minister Lyonchhen Tshering Tobgay. Modi was accompanied by External Affairs Minister Smt. Sushma Swaraj. India's relations with Bhutan are unique and especially warm. The two countries have historical and cultural linkages, which make them natural friends and partners.

India is providing ₹ 4,500 crore assistance to Bhutan for its economic development in areas of infrastructure, information and communication technology, health, agriculture, human resource development and tourism under its 11th Five Year Plan from 2013 to 2018.

But the hydropower cooperation between India and Bhutan is the most important feature. Bhutan with its hydropower projects can generate revenue for its economic development by selling power to India, which needs clean and low cost electricity. The three hydropower projects totaling 1416 MW are already operational and three more projects under construction are scheduled to be commissioned in 2017-18.

In April 2014, India and Bhutan had signed a framework agreement on four more joint venture model hydroelectric projects totaling 2120 MW. One of these projects, the 600 MW Kholongchu, located in Trashiyangtse in Eastern Bhutan, is a joint venture between the Indian and Bhutanese PSUs, the SJVN (Satluj Jal Vidyut Nigam) of India and DGPC (Druk Green Power Corporation) of Bhutan. During the visit, Modi unveiled the Foundation Stone of Kholongchu Hydropower Project.

The Prime Minister, Shri Narendra Modi at the lunch hosted by the King of Bhutan, His Majesty Jigme Khesar Namgyel Wangchuck, in Thimphu, Bhutan on June 16, 2014.

Modi also inaugurated the new Supreme Court building constructed with India's assistance at a cost of US$119.94 million.

In a statement that he had chosen Bhutan as his first visit abroad, the Prime Minister, before leaving for Bhutan, said, "*Relations with Bhutan will be a key foreign policy of my government...we are committed to continuing our unstinted support to Bhutan in its development effort.*"

The Prime Minister, Shri Narendra Modi meets people who lined up to say goodbye, waving flags, on way to the airport, in Thimphu, Bhutan on June 16, 2014.

Modi addressed the Joint Sitting of the Parliament in the Gyalyong Tshogkhang and held bilateral meetings with Bhutanese leaders. The highlights of the discussions were:

(i) India allocated Rs/Nu 45 billion for the 11th Five Year Plan and Rs/Nu 5 billion for the economic stimulus plan of the Royal Government of Bhutan.

The Prime Minister, Shri Narendra Modi unveiling the plaque to lay the foundation stone of Bhutan-India Cooperation Kholongchu Hydroelectric Project (600MW), in Thimphu, Bhutan on June 16, 2014. The Prime Minister of Bhutan, Mr. Lyonchhen Tshering Tobgay is also seen.

(ii) In the hydropower sector, the two countries expressed singular vision of achieving the 10,000 MW target. According to one estimate, India needs at least US$15 billion to raise the hydroelectric power of 10,000 MW in Bhutan.

(iii) India expressed its desire to exempt Bhutan from any ban or quantitative restrictions on exports of milk powder, wheat, edible oil, pulses and non-basmati rice.

(iv) In the education sector, Modi doubled the Nehru-Wangchuck scholarship to Rs/Nu 20 million per year and promised to provide grants for the National Library of Bhutan and also for all of Bhutan's 20 districts with a view to establish the digital section/E-library.

(v) On the issue of security, the two sides vowed not to allow each other's territory to be used for interests inimical to each other.

Modi said before his departure to Bhutan, "*People-to-people contact is an important aspect of our bilateral relations. I intend to discuss with the Bhutanese leadership how to further strengthen these contacts between our countries, particularly among the youth. In this regard, the role of educational links will be very important.*"

Modi's visit to Bhutan has given a fillip to further strengthening the close bonds of friendship and cooperation between the two countries.

The Prime Minister, Shri Narendra Modi meeting the King of Bhutan, His Majesty Jigme Khesar Namgyel Wangchuck, at Tashichhodzong Palace, in Thimphu, Bhutan on June 15, 2014.

Modi Visits NEPAL (August 3-4, 2014)

"Yes, we can do business in Nepal and still succeed. That is what I proved." —**Binod Chaudhary**, the first Nepali billionaire as listed by Forbes

Modi's next destination was Nepal, the Himalayan Kingdom, which was also characterised for more reasons than one. It was a visit by an Indian Prime Minister to this country after 17 years, the last being made by Shri IK Gujral in 1997. Here again Modi continued with his economic agenda focussing on India-funded hydroelectricity projects in Nepal and other infrastructure projects.

Modi called for frequent political engagement and closer cooperation *"across the full spectrum of our extraordinary broad-based relation, which will serve as a model and catalyst for South Asian partnership for prosperity,"* thus clearly showing his commitment to inclusive development of the region.

Modi was bestowed the privilege to be the first foreign leader to address the Nepalese Parliament. Establishing immediate rapport with Nepalese people, he visited the fifth century Pashupatinath Temple, performed puja, and donated ₹ 25 crore and 2,500 kilograms of sandalwood to the temple authority. Modi also announced a credit assistance programme of US$1 billion to Nepal.

Modi's Thrust on Power Generation

Fully understanding the need for more electricity for India's speedy industrialisation, Modi put forward his developmental agenda and said "*Nepal can free India of its darkness with its electricity...we don't want free electricity, we want to buy it. Just by selling electricity to India, Nepal can find a place in the developed countries of the world.*" He also assured the Nepali MPs (Members of Parliament) in a meeting that he wanted to turn India's "*hostile borders benign and ultimately gateways for free trade and commerce...borders must be bridges not barriers.*"

The Prime Minister, Shri Narendra Modi with the Prime Minister of Nepal, Shri Sushil Koirala releasing the commemorative stamps, at Chambers, PMO, Singha Darbar, in Kathmandu, Nepal on August 03, 2014.

The Prime Minister, Shri Narendra Modi and the Prime Minister of Nepal, Shri Sushil Koirala, at the delegation level talk, at Chambers, PMO, Singha Darbar, in Kathmandu, Nepal on August 03, 2014.

The meeting between Modi and his Nepalese counterpart, Sushil Koirala, reaffirmed the 'excellent' state of Nepal-India relations that encompass a broad spectrum of political, economic, social and cultural ties that are deep-rooted at both government and peoples' level. The two Prime Ministers also stressed the need to further explore ways to enhance sub-regional cooperation particularly in the areas of trade, transit, connectivity and hydropower.

India and Nepal had signed a Treaty of Peace and Friendship in 1950, which the two Prime Ministers agreed to review along with other bilateral agreements.

Both Modi and Koirala underlined the need to resolve pending Nepal-India boundary issues once for all. They welcomed the formation of the BWG (Boundary Working Group) to undertake the construction, restoration and repair of boundary pillars including clearance of 'No Man's Land' and other technical tasks.

Among the notable agreements listed below was the setting up of the Pancheshwar Development Authority within six months, so that work on the project could begin within a year.

The Prime Minister, Shri Narendra Modi at the Pashupatinath Temple, in Kathmandu, Nepal on August 04, 2014.

(i) It was decided to conclude negotiations within 45 days on the Project Development Agreement (PDA) between the Investment Board of Nepal and GMR Group of India for the development of Upper Karnali Hydropower Project.

(ii) A time period of 45 days was agreed upon to the concerned authorities by the two leaders to conclude negotiations on the agreement on trade in power sector. They also sought early conclusion of other three PDAs namely Arun III, Upper Marsyangdi and Tamakoshi III, development which, the two Prime Ministers felt, would be a major catalyst for the development of Nepal's enormous hydropower potential.

(iii) At the request of Nepal, India assured to assist the construction of a multilane motorable bridge over Mahakali River at Mahendranagar, which will allow traffic along the East-West Highway to cross over this river and establish a vital trade and transit linkage of far western region of Nepal with Indian cities of Uttar Pradesh, Delhi and Uttarakhand. Besides the two sides decided to consider construction of motorable bridges at the border points at Jhulaghat and Darchula.

(iv) It was also decided to expedite the construction of Postal roads and feeder roads (Terai roads) and complete the Phase I expeditiously and commence Phase II within a year.

(v) Expedite construction of cross border railway at all five agreed border points and the four Integrated Check Posts (ICPs) to facilitate cross border trade and transit as well as Nepal's export to and import from third countries.

(vi) India accepted Nepalese request to take up the project for the construction of Raxaul-Amlekhgunj petroleum pipeline in the first phase and extend it to Kathmandu in the next phase to facilitate the transport of petroleum products.

Modi's Second Visit to NEPAL (November 25 to 27, 2014)

"Actually Nepal and India are not two countries"
—**BP Koirala**, Former Prime Minister of Nepal

Within a span of six months, Modi again visited Nepal in November 2014 to attend the 18th SAARC summit in Kathmandu from November 25 to 27.

The Prime Minister, Shri Narendra Modi handing over the Dhruv ALH to Nepal Army, at Army Pavilion, in Kathmandu, Nepal, on November 25, 2014. The Union Minister for External Affairs and Overseas Indian Affairs, Smt. Sushma Swaraj is also seen.

The Prime Minister, Shri Narendra Modi and the Prime Minister of Nepal, Shri Sushil Koirala, at the official handover and inaugural ceremony of the National Trauma Centre, in Kathmandu, Nepal on November 25, 2014.

On the sidelines of SAARC Summit, Modi held bilateral meeting with his Nepalese counterpart, Koirala. The notable outcomes of the visit were as many as 16 agreements in various fields, ranging from hydropower projects, road connectivity, tourism, health to defence cooperation. These include:

(i) Signing of Memorandum of Understanding (MoU) on Motor Vehicle Agreement and flagging off Kathmandu-Delhi bus service 'Pashupatinath Express' by Modi. This bus service that will initially run between Kathmandu-New Delhi, Kathmandu-Varanasi and Pokhara-New Delhi, will help the people of both the countries in trouble-free crossing of the border.

(ii) Signing of MoU on construction of National Police Academy at Panauti, 32 km south-east of Kathmandu, with India's funding of ₹ 550 crore.

(iii) Line of Credit of US$1 billion from EXIM Bank to Nepal Government for hydropower projects, irrigation and infrastructural development projects as announced by Modi during his visit to Nepal earlier in August 2014.

(iv) Supply of one Dhruv ALH (Advanced Light Helicopter) Mark III to Nepal Army. Dhruv ALH named after the polestar is a light 5.5 tonne class multirole and multi-mission helicopter, designed and developed by HAL (Hindustan Aeronautics Limited).

It is also significant that Modi demonstrated his commitment towards Nepal and won the hearts of the people of that country when Nepal was struck by a series of earthquakes. Without even waiting for a formal call for assistance from Nepal, he ordered immediate relief and sent various teams to Nepal for rescue operations.

Modi in SRI LANKA (March 13-14, 2015)

"An economically peaceful and prosperous Sri Lanka is the dream of youth of the nation. My message for the youth is to collectively work for an inclusively developed Sri Lanka."

—**APJ Abdul Kalam**, Late President of India

Modi's address to the Sri Lankan Parliament said it all, *"India and Sri Lanka are too close to look away from each other. Nor can we be insulated from one another. Our recent histories have shown that we suffer together, and we are more effective when we work together. The Indian Ocean is critical to the security and prosperity of our two countries. And, we can be more successful in achieving the goals if we work together; build a climate of trust and confidence; and, remain sensitive to each other's interests. Our partnership will be vital for building a peaceful, secure, stable and prosperous maritime neighbourhood."*

Modi was the first Indian Prime Minister to pay a bilateral visit to Sri Lanka in 28 years. The visit strengthened the belief that India can play a meaningful role in enhancing Sri Lanka's development prospects. Certain new developments have made conditions ideal for strengthening Indo-Sri Lanka economic reforms.

There is little doubt that India has reworked its equation with its immediate neighbours and has concluded that for own development and for pursuing global ambitions, there is no alternative to peace and prosperity in the region. A case in point are the neighbouring countries of Bangladesh, Bhutan and Nepal that have capitalised on this in various sectors, including power generation, grid connectivity, improved road and rail transport, thereby boosting trade.

With India becoming the fastest growing economy in the world, Modi has urged Sri Lanka to participate in India's sustained forward march that has resulted from a combination of a reform-oriented government and demographic dynamics. There is little doubt that opportunities are likely to materialise for countries in the sub-region, including Sri Lanka, due to greater dynamism in the Indian economy.

Taking a leaf out of the experience of East and South East Asia, where the rise of both Japan and China furthered the prosperity in the countries of that region through the growth of manufacturing supply chains, Modi's 'Make-in-India' strategy promises to replicate their experience in its own region.

What goes in favour of Sri Lanka and India is the proximity to each other that enables improved infrastructure and strengthens enabling conditions for both to take full advantage. Previously, the economies of the two countries remained distant due to poor infrastructure that shot up the transaction costs, but now improved conditions in terms of better roads, ports and railways offer ideal conditions for supply chain driven growth in trade and investment for both.

Modi began his day-long tour by greeting the people of Sri Lanka with "*Ayubhuvan, Vanakkam and Salaam,*" and was immediately at home with the Sri Lankans. Besides holding bilateral meetings, he addressed the Sri Lankan Parliament and Business Community in Colombo on March 13, 2015.

Addressing the Sri Lankan Parliament, Modi said that the future of a country is influenced by the state of its neighbourhood. He said, "*The future that I dream for India is also the future that*

The Prime Minister of Sri Lanka, Shri Ranil Wickremesinghe meeting the Prime Minister, Shri Narendra Modi, in Colombo, Sri Lanka on March 13, 2015.

The Prime Minister, Shri Narendra Modi being presented a memento, at the business meeting hosted by the Ceylon Chamber of Commerce, in Colombo, Sri Lanka on March 13, 2015.

I wish for our neighbours. India and Sri Lanka have civilisational links, even though the two countries don't have a boundary, but are the closest neighbours in every sense. No matter where you look in India and Sri Lanka, the many strands of our links—religion, language, culture, food, customs, traditions and epics—come together into a deep and strong bond of familiarity and friendship."

He said that Sri Lanka's success in economic field, progress and prosperity is vital for India and the future of Indian Ocean region. He praised Sri Lanka for its cooperation in South Asia.

Tamil Issue

Indirectly touching the sensitive Tamilian issue in Sri Lanka, Modi said, "*Diversity could be a source of strength for a nation and I am a strong believer in cooperative federalism.*" He further added, "*Sri Lanka has lived through decades of tragic violence and conflict. You have successfully defeated terrorism and brought the conflict to an end....*"

The recent conclusion of election has also reflected the hope for change, reconciliation and unity. Modi asserted, "*We stand with you in your efforts to build a future that accommodates the aspirations of all sections of society, including the Sri Lankan Tamil community, for a life of equality, justice, peace and dignity in a united Sri Lanka.*"

Modi's Inclusive Agenda of Development

Pursuing his 'Neighbourhood First' Policy and inclusive economic agenda, Modi said his vision of an ideal neighbourhood is one in which trade, investments, technology, ideas and people flow easily across borders.

He said India was now the fastest growing economy in the world which sees India as the new destination for economic opportunity. But the neighbours should have the first claim on India, which could serve as a catalyst in the progress of its neighbour. He conveyed India's willingness to address their concern to boost trade and make it more balanced. Present trade between the two countries was more favourable to India.

Stressing the need for a comprehensive Economic Partnership Agreement between the two countries, Modi said India could be a natural source of investments in Sri Lanka; for exports to India and elsewhere; and to build infrastructure. He said, "*We can also work together to harness the vast potential of the Ocean economy.*"

The Prime Minister, Shri Narendra Modi visiting the Mahabodhi Society Temple, in Colombo, Sri Lanka on March 13, 2015.

Regional Cooperation

Modi suggested that India and Sri Lanka could lead in increasing cooperation in the South Asian region and the linked 'BIMSTEC (Bay of Bengal Initiative for Multi-Sectoral Technical and Economic Cooperation)' region, and asked Sri Lanka to take full benefit of India's satellite for the SAARC region.

India, he said, had committed US$ 1.6 billion in development assistance to Sri Lanka and up to US$318 million to the railway sector. Other potential areas of cooperation between the two countries could be agriculture, education, health, science & technology and space.

People-to-People Contact

Modi referred to India's decision to extend visa on arrival facility to Sri Lankan citizens which will increase connectivity between the two countries. Besides, India had reduced fees for Sri Lankans visiting National Museum in Delhi.

Terrorism

Expressing concern over terrorism and extremism, which were posing threats in new forms and from new sources the world over, he said that the need for cooperation to check such activities was stronger today. Modi maintained that the Indian Ocean was critical to the security and prosperity of both the countries. Maritime security cooperation between India, Sri Lanka and Maldives needs to be widened to include other countries in the Indian Ocean area.

The Prime Minister, Shri Narendra Modi offering prayers at the Naguleswaram Temple, in Jaffna, Sri Lanka on March 14, 2015.

Following is the outcome of Modi's visit to Sri Lanka:

(i) To further strengthen Sri Lanka's foreign exchange position steps have been initiated to supplement its external reserves by the Swap arrangement (US$400 million) between the CBSL (Central Bank of Sri Lanka) and RBI (Reserve Bank of India).

(ii) A sum of US$320 million has been made available for Sri Lanka's railway development. This will improve the connectivity between the hinterland and major cities, as also ports and airports to facilitate the movement of goods.

(iii) Steps have been taken to improve energy security by establishing the Sampur coal based electricity generation facility and by developing Trincomalee Tank Farms to increase the utilisation of this underperforming entity.

India becoming Sri Lanka's biggest trading partner and largest source of FDI in recent years has resulted from the Indo-Lanka FTA, despite all the difficulties encountered. With FTA being the most competitive component of Sri Lanka's economy, this builds a strong case for extending the current FTA to include services. India is willing to accept the principle of non-reciprocity and is game to opening up much more than Sri Lanka. On ground, Sri Lanka, under the existing laws, such as the Board of Investment Act, will liberalise very few items bound by the said laws.

Despite India sending the highest number of tourists to Sri Lanka, there is a considerable scope not only to increase the numbers, but also the daily spend per head. This is because of the improvement of its hotel inventory and customised products, such as the Ramayana Trail. Scope also exists to expand transportation and improve grid connectivity of air and ferry services.

India's new liberalised visa regime, announced by Modi during his visit to Sri Lanka and implemented on April 14, 2015, is bound to benefit people-to-people contact, as well as business for the Sri Lankans.

Significant benefits accrue for both India and Sri Lanka through expanded Indo-Lanka bilateral economic relations. This translates into increased trade, investment, training, technology and markets for Sri Lanka. For India, it offers a more prosperous neighborhood that both boosts its development and helps it to focus on its global agenda.

Modi in BANGLADESH (June 6-7, 2015)

"We have to get out of this mindset that the rich will do the business and the poor will have the charity."—**Muhammed Yunus**, Nobel Laureate and Founder of Grameen Bank

Indo-Bangladesh Relations

"We are not just neighbours. We are two nations bound by the threads of history, religion, culture, language and kinship, and, of course, the passion for cricket.... As our economies get more integrated and our people better connected, our nations will become more prosperous. It will also open new economic doors for India's Northeast. And it will enable our two countries to integrate South Asia and connect it with the dynamic East," said Modi, after signing the agreement with Bangladesh to resolve the border issue.

India was the first country to recognise Bangladesh as a separate and independent state, and established diplomatic relations with that country immediately after its independence in December 1971. The two countries have common heritage, linguistic and cultural ties. Therefore, India has cultural, social and economic links with Bangladesh.

The Prime Minister, Shri Narendra Modi meeting the presidents of leading Chambers of Commerce and Industry in Dhaka, Bangladesh on June 07, 2015.

The geographical locations of the two countries complement each other and present an opportunity for both to further develop their connectivity links and economies. Bangladesh holds importance for Modi's 'Act East' Policy, since both the countries are included in several groups that aim to expand connectivity between South Asia, and South East Asia and China. This constitutes a number of initiatives that include the Mekong Ganga Cooperative Initiative, BIMSTEC (Bay of Bengal Initiative for multi-sectoral technical and economic cooperation) and the BCIM (Bangladesh-China-India-Myanmar) economic corridor project. The relations between the two South Asian neighbours significantly improved in the past decade.

The visits of Bangladesh Prime Minister, Sheikh Hasina to India in January 2010 and then of Indian PM Manmohan Singh to Bangladesh in September 2011 opened a new chapter in India's bilateral relations with Bangladesh. Besides, President Pranab Mukherjee's visit to Bangladesh in March 2013, on his first trip abroad since assuming the office, proved the Indian Government is according the highest importance to its relationship with Bangladesh based on the principles of equality, partnership and mutual growth.

Sushma Swaraj's first 'stand-alone' visit to Bangladesh as the External Affairs Minister in June 2014, also provided further momentum to the close and friendly relationship of the two countries.

In over four decades, the two countries have continued to consolidate their political, economic, trade and cultural relations and have built a comprehensive institutional framework to promote bilateral cooperation. Both countries share 54 rivers, out of which, a treaty is already in existence for sharing of the Ganga waters and both sides are working for early finalisation of agreements for sharing of water of other common rivers. Both countries are also cooperating in the conservation of the entire Sunderbans ecosystem, which is a common biodiversity heritage.

Bangladesh is an important trading partner for India. The two way trade in fiscal 2012-2013 was reported to be US$5.34 billion with India's exports to Bangladesh accounting for US$4.776 billion and imports US$0.564 million with the duty free access to Bangladesh by India for most items.

Investment by Indian companies in Bangladesh continues to grow with the signing of bilateral Investment Promotion and Protection agreement.

For the first time in their post-independence history, India and Bangladesh have established inter-grid connectivity for the flow of bulk power from India to Bangladesh. Prime Ministers of both the countries inaugurated the grid connectivity.

Bangladesh has started importing 500 MW Power from India since October 2013. India has always stood by Bangladesh in its hour of need with aid and economic assistance to help it cope with natural disasters and floods.

Bangladesh is a recipient of US$800 million from India as a line of credit for numerous projects that include railway infrastructure, supply of broad gauge microprocessor-based locomotives and passenger coaches, procurement of buses and dredging projects. Of this line of credit, US$150 million out of the US$200 million grant has already been released to Bangladesh in three installments for priority projects.

India and Bangladesh are also engaged in regional cooperation through multilateral forum such as SAARC (South Asian Association for Regional Cooperation), BIMSTEC (Bay of Bengal Multi-Sectoral Technical and Economic Cooperation) and IOR-ARC (Indian Ocean Rim Association for Regional Cooperation), etc. In pursuance of directions of the Prime Ministers of India and Bangladesh, both sides have also commenced implementation of sub-regional cooperation initiatives along with Nepal and Bhutan.

State Visit to Bangladesh

Keeping in line with his 'Neighbours First' policy, Prime Minister Modi embarked on a two-day visit to Bangladesh on June 6, 2015, primarily to oversee the protocol for exchange of instrument of ratification for India-Bangladesh Land Boundary Agreement, 1974 and its 2011 Protocol, a dispute lingering for long. Parliament of India has put its seal on the Agreement on May 7, 2014 during the Manmohan Singh government.

In Modi's own words, "*Our Parliament's approval of Land Boundary Agreement reflects the consensus in India on relations with Bangladesh. The visit is at a historic moment. We have resolved a question that has lingered since Independence. Our two nations have a settled boundary. It will make our borders more secure and people's life there more stable.*" India-Bangladesh accord on the settlement of the maritime boundary last year was also testimony to the maturity of the ties between the two countries and their shared commitment to international rules.

Modi took no time to develop rapport with the people by his tribute to 'Bangabandhu' Sheikh Mujib-ur-Rahman, describing him as great leader of this era. He said, "*His vision and leadership, his humanism and sacrifices, gave birth to the dream of 'Sonar Bangla'. Today that dream prospers through the leadership of Prime Minister Sheikh Hasina and the genius of the people of Bangladesh.*"

He talked about his deeply held belief in the shared prosperity of neighbours and said the economies of both the countries got more integrated and with the people better connected, both the countries would become more prosperous.

Bus Service

Modi referred to the two bus services jointly launched on June 6 by him, Bangladesh PM Sheikh Hasina and West Bengal Chief Minister Mamata Banerjee between India and Bangladesh, which would take people-to-people contact to a new horizon. "*Better relations between the two countries would open new economic doors for India's Northeast region, besides enabling India and Bangladesh to integrate South Asia and connect it with the dynamic East*", he said.

Modi's commitment to peace in the region was reflected in his observations that India and Bangladesh were the largest contributors to United Nations Peacekeeping initiative. The two countries can also make the region safer and more prosperous, and the seas more secure. The observation can also be seen in the context of his inclusive economic agenda which could only be achieved when there is complete peace and tranquillity in the region.

Land Boundary

Protocol for Exchange of Instrument of Ratification for Land Boundary Agreement was among the 22 Agreements, MoUs and other documents concluded during the visit.

This also included the Coastal Shipping Agreement intended to boost bilateral trade. The Indian Economic Zone will promote Indian investments in Bangladesh. The agreement on blue economy and maritime cooperation will also open new area of economic opportunities. Besides, the new border haat at Kamalasagar will reinforce traditional economic links.

Modi also responded positively on Bangladesh's concern over huge trade imbalance. "*We will do everything we can to bridge the deficit. Indian investments in Bangladesh will help. I will also try to make trade smoother and easier, including at the border. The agreement on standards and testing is a step in that direction.*"

The Prime Minister, Shri Narendra Modi with the President of Bangladesh, Mr. Abdul Hamid and the Prime Minister of Bangladesh, Ms. Sheikh Hasina, at Bangabhaban, in Dhaka, Bangladesh on June 07, 2015.

Power

Modi also assured Bangladesh of augmenting the power supply from 500 MW to 1100 MW within two years and said the two countries can do more together in power sector, while referring to the progress of the 1320 MW Rampal Power Project between the two countries.

Credit Line

On development partnership between the two countries, Modi announced another line of credit of US$2 billion to support infrastructure and other development activities in Bangladesh and added that the quick implementation of the line of credit of US$800 million and full disbursement of US$200 million in grant was *"a tribute to our cooperation."*

Teesta River Discord

In the context of the Teesta River water discord and on which the two countries failed to reach any agreement, Modi said, "*Our rivers should nurture our relationship, not become a source of discord. Water sharing is above all, a human issue. It affects life and livelihood on both sides of the border.*"

He added, "*We have shown political resolve and mutual goodwill with the Land Boundary Agreement and I am confident that with the support of state governments in India, we can reach a fair solution on Teesta and Feni Rivers.*"

Joint Declaration between Bangladesh and India

The talks of the two Prime Ministers became a platform for both Modi and Hasina to reminisce the shared commonalities between the two countries in context of their history, tradition, and the like. This firmed their conviction to further reinforce the bilateral relations to foster peace, development and stability for the peoples of the two countries. Acknowledging the new phase of bilateral relations, the two Prime Ministers vowed to adopt a pragmatic, mature and practical approach for the mutual benefit of their people and collective prosperity of the region.

Both the Prime Ministers described the 'historic' passage of the Land Boundary Agreement by the Indian Parliament a milestone in the relations of the two countries.

The 'Framework Agreement on Cooperation for Development' of 2011 was recalled by the two leaders. This framework outlines the shared vision for long-term cooperation and envisages closer ties through economic integration and better connectivity.

The two leaders expressed satisfaction in continued exchange of high level visits and wished more such high level interactions between the two sides that will help achieve a better understanding on many of the issues under discussion.

Appreciating the progress made in the 3rd meeting of JCC (Joint Consultative Commission) held in New Delhi on September 20, 2014, the two leaders directed their respective Ministers of Foreign/External Affairs to coordinate and follow up the implementation of initiatives as also to explore fresh avenues for cooperation. They jointly agreed to hold the 4th meeting of the JCC in 2015 in Dhaka.

The two leaders not only expressed satisfaction at the level of cooperation between the two countries on security issues, but also reaffirmed their uncompromising position against extremism and terrorism in all forms. They committed to cooperate with each other through sharing terrorism-related information and pledged not to permit their respective territories to be used for any activity inimical to the other.

Modi expressed India's appreciation for the cooperation extended by Bangladesh in security related matters. The two Prime Ministers expressed satisfaction at the conclusion of the MoUs on Prevention of Smuggling of Fake Currency Notes, cooperation between Coast Guards and Prevention of Human Trafficking, all of which will augment security cooperation.

The need for effective implementation of CBMP (Coordinated Border Management Plan) for better border management was expressed by the two leaders. This is to prevent cross border criminal and violent activities and tragic loss of lives. This Plan will enhance cooperation between the border forces of the two countries to prevent criminal activities, etc. along the border areas.

Both the Prime Ministers stressed on the importance of finalising the Standard Operating Procedures (SOPs) for Indian border roads for construction and maintenance of Border Out Posts (BOPs) of the Border Guards Bangladesh. This also includes the use of Indian medical facilities in difficult border areas by Bangladeshi personnel deployed in the vicinity. Both the leaders took the common view of bringing down the deaths on both sides to zero and directed the concerned authorities to work to that effect. The first round of meetings of DCs/DMs of bordering districts was welcomed by the two leaders, who expressed their desire to hold such meetings on a regular basis.

On the request of Prime Minister Hasina for jointly developing the Ganges Barrage on the river Padma in Bangladesh, Modi assured to get the issue examined by the concerned Indian agencies.

Reminding Modi of Interim Agreement on Sharing of the Water of Teesta inked between the two governments in January 2011, Prime Minister Hasina requested early conclusion of the same. Modi assured her of the same after due deliberations involving all the stakeholders on sharing of waters of Teesta and Feni at the earliest.

The two leaders also discussed sharing of waters of the Manu, Muhuri, Khowai, Gumti, Dharla and Dudhkumar rivers and directed the concerned officials under JRC (Joint Research Centre) to take expeditious action.

Power Generation

Expressing complete satisfaction in cooperation and achievements in the power sector between the two countries, the two leaders agreed to further expand their cooperation. Modi appreciated PM Hasina for making efforts for achieving installed capacity of 24,000 MW power by the year 2021 and assured her of India playing a major role in achieving this goal with the help of many Indian corporates. To this end, he asked Prime Minister Hasina to facilitate the entry of Indian companies in the power generation, transmission and distribution sector of Bangladesh. The two leaders also decided to boost the power supply from 500 MW to 1,000 MW through the Bheramara-Baharampur grid inter-connection and put in operation supply of 100 MW power from India, including that from Palatana Power Plant to eastern Bangladesh.

A consensus reached between Bangladesh and India to evacuate power from the North-Eastern India's Rangia/Rowta region to Muzaffarnagar through Bangladesh constructing a 7000 MW DC grid line with suitable power tapping points at Barapukuria in Bangladesh was welcomed by the two leaders. Modi assured his Bangladesh counterpart of providing adequate power from this line to Bangladesh.

Modi also agreed to enhance cooperation in renewable energy and nuclear energy sectors. Both the leaders agreed to cooperate in the field of civil nuclear energy, especially in training technical personnel.

The growing cooperation between the two countries in the energy sector encouraged the two sides to initiate an annual India-Bangladesh Energy Dialogue to be led jointly by Secretary (Petroleum) of India and Secretary, Power Division of Bangladesh. This will facilitate undertaking comprehensive energy sector cooperation including areas of coal, natural gas, LNG (Liquefied Natural Gas), supply of petroleum products, renewable energy, oil and gas pipelines, etc.

Both the leaders agreed to ensure unfettered bilateral trade by eliminating hurdles to trade. They stressed the need to narrow trade imbalance between the two countries and acknowledged the conclusion of the Bilateral Cooperation Agreement between BSTI (Bangladesh Standards and Testing Institute) and BIS (Bureau of Indian Standards).

Special Economic Zones for India

Modi lauded Bangladesh for allocating land for SEZs (Special Economic Zones) for India, while highlighting the role of the private sector. Both the Prime Ministers welcomed the MoU (Memorandum of Understanding) for Establishment of Indian SEZs in Bangladesh.

Giving emphasis to regional economic development and people-to-people contact through seamless, multi-modal connectivity, both Modi and Hasina emphasised the importance of roadways, railways and waterways for an inter-dependent and mutually beneficial relationship among the countries of the region. They also laid the groundwork for negotiations on a Multi Modal Transport Agreement between the two countries and agreed to constitute a Joint Task Force for this purpose.

Train Connectivity

Bangladesh's proposal for considering introduction of second Maitree Express between Khulna and Kolkata was accepted by Modi, as the two leaders expressed happiness over the ongoing cooperation in the railways sector.

A second Line of Credit worth US$2 billion was offered to Bangladesh by Modi for various development projects that include public transport, roads, railways, inland waterways, ports, IT (Information Technology), education, health, etc.

Emphasising the importance of sub-regional cooperation in power sector, water resources, trade, transit and connectivity, the two Prime Ministers expressed the need to harness them for mutual benefit.

The Prime Minister, Shri Narendra Modi visits Ramakrishna Mission, in Dhaka, Bangladesh on June 07, 2015.

Climate Change

The two Prime Ministers recognised the need to exploit the synergies between the two countries in new areas that include nuclear science & technology, space, health, jute & textiles, renewable energy, fisheries, meteorological and other areas.

Maritime Cooperation

Hailing the amicable settlement of the maritime boundary between the two countries, the two leaders expressed their desire to develop ocean-based Blue Economy and Maritime Cooperation in the Bay of Bengal and also to chart out the ways for future cooperation.

Admitting climate change as one of the greatest challenges facing mankind today, the two leaders emphasised on working in tandem with other countries for arriving at a comprehensive and equitable climate agreement in Paris in 2015, which also addresses technology collaboration and financial support in meeting this common global challenge. An agreement to intensify bilateral cooperation in the areas of climate change and environment protection was reached between the two.

The two Prime Ministers recognised the ongoing cooperation between the two countries in education and endorsed to cement this cooperation through collaborative arrangements between the universities and educational institutes of both the countries for mutual benefit.

Expressing happiness over the growing exchanges between the peoples of the two countries, which is helping foster greater understanding and goodwill, the two leaders agreed to give a further boost to people-to-people contacts. An agreement between Doordarshan and BTV (Bangladesh Television) to allow BTV to join Prasar Bharati's DTH (Direct to Home) platform was envisaged by the two leaders.

Cooperation at Multilateral Forums

The two Prime Ministers reviewed the steps taken to work closely for regional/sub-regional cooperation, including SAARC, BIMSTEC and BCIM-EC (Bangladesh, India, China and Myanmar-Economic Corridor). Welcoming the agreement on establishing of the BIMSTEC electricity grid, the two leaders hoped for early finalisation of the BIMSTEC Free Trade Agreement.

Emphasising the importance of working in close proximity in the UN multi-lateral organisations, the two leaders reiterated the importance of coordinating their positions on the emerging global development architecture including Post-2015 Development

Agenda, Migration and Development, and other multi-lateral issues of common interest.

Acknowledging a strong United Nations, as a key factor in tackling global challenges, both the Prime Ministers highlighted the importance of an effective multilateral system. They expressed unhappiness at the slow pace on the long standing subject of UN Security Council Reform and called for urgent progress in the 70th anniversary year of the United Nations. To this end, Bangladesh fully backed India's candidature for permanent membership of an expanded and reformed UN Security Council.

The Prime Minister, Shri Narendra Modi paying homage to "Bangabandhu" Sheikh Mujib-ur Rahman, at Bangabandhu Memorial Museum, in Dhanmondi, Dhaka on June 06, 2015.

Multilateral financial institutions need strengthening and reform was accepted by both the Prime Ministers. They rooted for the participation of developing countries in international economic decision-making and expressed happiness over the role the New Development Bank and the Asian Infrastructure Investment Bank may play in response to the needs of the developing countries. Bangladesh's desire to become a member of the New Development Bank in due course was noted by Modi.

Bilateral documents which were signed, exchanged, adopted and handed over during the visit include:

(i) Exchange of Instruments of Ratification of 1974 Land Boundary Agreement and its 2011 Protocol.

(ii) Exchange of letters on Modalities for implementation of 1974 Land and Boundary Agreement and its 2011 Protocol.

(iii) Bilateral Trade Agreement (renewal).

(iv) Agreement on Coastal Shipping between Bangladesh and India.

(v) Protocol on Inland Water Transit and Trade (renewal).

(vi) Bilateral Cooperation Agreement between BSTI and BIS on Cooperation in the field of Standardisation.

(vii) Agreement on Dhaka-Shillong-Guwahati Bus Service and its Protocol.

(viii) Agreement on Kolkata-Dhaka-Agartala Bus Service and its Protocol.

(ix) Memorandum of Understanding between Coast Guards.

(x) Memorandum of Understanding on Prevention of Human Trafficking.

(xi) Memorandum of Understanding on Prevention of Smuggling and Circulation of Fake Currency Notes.

(xii) Memorandum of Understanding between Bangladesh and India for Extending a New LoC (Line of Credit) of US$2 billion by Government of India to Government of Bangladesh.

(xiii) Memorandum of Understanding on Blue Economy and Maritime Cooperation in the Bay of Bengal and the Indian Ocean.

(xiv) Memorandum of Understanding on Use of Chittagong and Mongla Ports.

(xv) Memorandum of Understanding for a Project under IECC (India Endowment for Climate Change).

(xvi) Memorandum of Understanding on Indian Economic Zone.

(xvii) Cultural Exchange Programme for the years 2015-17.

(xviii) Statement of Intent on Bangladesh-India Education Cooperation (adoption).

(xix) Agreement between BSCCL (Bangladesh Submarine Cable Company Limited) and BSNL (Bharat Sanchar Nigam Limited) for leasing of international bandwidth for internet at Akhaura.

MYANMAR: India and ASEAN (November 11-13, 2014)

"With the right kind of institutions, starting with the rule of law, Burma could progress very quickly."

—**Aung San Suu Kyi**, Nobel Laureate and President of the National League for Democracy in Myanmar

Background

Commerce, culture and connectivity are the three pillars of India's engagement with ASEAN which has invested about

US$27.9 billion in India over the past eight years, against India's investments in ASEAN amounting to US$32.4 billion over the period. India-ASEAN trade is around US$76 billion catering to a combined market of 1.8 billion people. However India's trade with ASEAN is just three per cent of total ASEAN trade. The two sides have set a target of US$100 billion for bilateral trade by 2015.

India has been in the forefront for giving fillip to numerous trans-national projects to lay the network of road, rail and maritime links to enhance connectivity. To this end, the Tamu-Kalewa-Kalemyo sector of the Indian-Myanmar-Thailand Tri-lateral Highway is set to promote India's multifaceted ties with the region.

The focus of Modi's government on North-Eastern states, the gateway to ASEAN, for giving economic boost, is set to infuse a new prosperity in this region.

Visiting Myanmar to attend his first India-ASEAN Summit and the 18-nation East Asia Summit, Modi took this golden opportunity to tell about India's 'Act East' policy that has replaced the previous 'Look East' policy.

Modi clarified in his opening statement at the 12th Indian-ASEAN Summit, why his government had redefined the policy. Unfolding his inclusive economic agenda, he said that a new era of economic development, industrialisation and trade had begun in India and his government had converted the 'Look East' Policy into the 'Act East' policy to make the policy proactive.

Modi said there are many similarities and convergences among ASEAN countries, majority of them belong to the developing world. Population wise India and ASEAN are second and third, and witnessing growing economies.

The Prime Minister, Shri Narendra Modi meeting the Chairperson and General Secretary of the National League for Democracy, Myanmar, Daw Aung San Suu Kyi, in Nay Pyi Taw, Myanmar on November 12, 2014.

"The ASEAN community is India's neighbour. We have ancient relations of trade, religion, culture, art and traditions. We have enriched each other through our interaction. This constitutes a strong foundation of a modern relationship," he said in Myanmar capital, Nay Pyi Taw.

"My government has been in office for six months and the intensity and momentum with which we have enhanced our engagement in the East, is a reflection of the priority that we give to this region," he told the Summit on the second day of his 10-day three-nation tour of Myanmar, Australia and Fiji.

India, with its population of 800 million people under 35 years, has set out on a new economic journey with a brand new 'Make in India' mission that focuses on infrastructure, manufacturing, trade, agriculture, skill development, urban renewal and smart cities. Steps have been taken to ease doing business in India and making policies attractive.

The Prime Minister, Shri Narendra Modi calling on the President of Myanmar, Mr. U. Thein Sein, at Nay Pyi Taw, Myanmar on November 11, 2014.

"*I invite you to this new environment in India. Indian companies are also keen to invest and trade with* ASEAN," Modi said, while adding that rapidly developing India and ASEAN can be great partners for each other. He said, "*We are both keen to enhance our cooperation in advancing balance, peace and stability in the region. But our potential is much higher than where we are at the moment.*"

"*Today,* ASEAN *has established its own identity and voice in global political and economic affairs. Today, the entire Asia-Pacific region desires integration and cooperation. To achieve this goal we look at* ASEAN, *not only for inspiration but also for its leadership; and you have achieved a great deal of success in leading us in that direction,*" he added.

The Prime Minister, Shri Narendra Modi with the President of Myanmar, Mr. U. Thein Sein and his wife Mrs. Khin Khin Win, at Gala Dinner of ASEAN and related summits, in Nay Pyi Taw, Myanmar on November 12, 2014.

The Prime Minister however asked ASEAN to review and further improve its free trade agreement on goods to benefit all. He also stressed the need to bring the FTA on Service and Investment into force at the earliest.

Referring to the Regional Comprehensive Economic Partnership Agreement about which many leaders had spoken, he agreed that this could be a 'springboard' for economic integration and prosperity in the region. He added, *"But we should aim for a balanced Agreement, which is beneficial to all; and, is truly comprehensive in nature, by equally ambitious agenda with similar timelines for goods and services."*

The Prime Minister, Shri Narendra Modi meeting the members of the Indian Community, in Nay Pyi Taw, Myanmar on November 13, 2014.

Modi said he was considering establishing a special facility or Special Purpose Vehicle with ASEAN cooperation to facilitate project financing and quick implementation and to enhance connectivity, but added that in this age, more than physical connectivity. We need information highways or i-ways. My experience is that even where road connectivity is poor, we can create vast economic opportunities and employment through i-ways. India is prepared to provide all assistance and cooperation in this area.

Seeking their cooperation and investments, the Prime Minister elaborated on his thrust areas plan to develop 100 smart cities and renewal of 500 cities, solar energy project, renewal energy and energy efficiency, science & technology, education, space science, health, including traditional medicine, climate change and environment and forests, agriculture and food security, skill development for creating job opportunities in addition to people to people contact through tourism and exchange of delegations.

"Space science can give us benefit in many sectors. We should quickly establish the new India-ASEAN space-related ground station in Vietnam and start the project for upgrading the existing station in Indonesia," Modi suggested.

On incidents of terrorism in many parts of the world, Modi praised the cooperation between ASEAN countries but stressed the need to further strengthen ties for countering terrorism, extremism, drugs, arms, and money laundering.

For maritime trade and passage, he said maritime security was very important and emphasized the need to follow international law and norms on maritime issues as it is done for air passage. Modi specifically spoke about the peace and stability in South China Sea and hoped that the code of conduct as per the 2002 guidelines could be concluded soon on South China Sea on the basis of consensus.

The Ninth East Asia Summit was held in Nay Pyi Taw, Myanmar, on November 12 and 13, 2014, which is an annual feature of national leaders from the East Asian region and adjoining countries.

All the countries supported the Summit Declaration on Islamic state (terror group). These nations, however, asserted that an international partnership was required for a comprehensive response against terrorism. The Summit rejected any linkage between religion and terrorism. They however stressed the need to ensure that cyberspace remain a source of connectivity and prosperity and not new threats of conflicts.

CHAPTER 2

'ACT EAST' POLICY

Modi's Visits to Japan, China, Mongolia and South Korea

Replacing India's 'Look East' Policy with 'Act East' Policy, Prime Minister Modi made it very clear that his Government would focus more and more on improving relations with ASEAN and other East Asian countries. The 'Look East' Policy was formulated during PV Narasimha Rao's government in 1992 for better economic engagement with its eastern neighbours. This policy has now been replaced with 'Act East' Policy for a more proactive role for India in this region.

Modi undertook visits to Japan, China, South Korea and Mongolia, seeking better trade relations and foreign investments in key sectors, like infrastructure and manufacturing.

Modi's Visit to JAPAN (August 30 to September 3, 2014)

"Japan never considers time together as time wasted. Rather, it is time invested." —**Donald Richie**

"India and Japan are Asia's two largest and oldest democracies, with ancient cultural links and enduring goodwill between their people. The two countries are joined together by convergent

global interests, critical maritime inter-connection and growing international responsibilities. They share an abiding commitment to peace and stability, international rule of law and open global trade regime.

Varanasi-Kyoto Partner City agreement signed in the presence of the Prime Minister, Shri Narendra Modi and the Prime Minister of Japan, Mr. Shinzo Abe, in Kyoto, Japan on August 30, 2014.

Their economies have vast complementarities that create boundless opportunities for mutually beneficial economic partnership," endorsed PM Modi and Japanese PM Shinzo Abe.

Modi chose Japan as his first destination outside the immediate neighbourhood to demonstrate how important Japan is in India's foreign and economic policies. Japan is of paramount importance for India to realise its 'Make in India' dream and also for peace, stability and prosperity of India, in particular and Asia, at large. Japan remains one of India's closest partners from political, economic, cultural and security points of view. The two countries are linked to each other through heritage with thread of Buddhism binding both.

Modi had visited Japan twice earlier as Chief Minister of Gujarat and therefore he had good relationship with the industrialists and political leadership of Japan. Japan has been the partner country for 'Vibrant Gujarat' summits all these years.

The fact that Modi spent five days in an Asian country signified the special ties, which the two vibrant democracies and leading economies of Asia enjoy. Modi visited Japan from August 30 to September 3, 2014 on the occasion of annual meeting between the two Prime Ministers.

Japanese Prime Minister Shinzo Abe was invited as the Chief Guest at the Republic Day celebrations on January 26, 2015. Both Modi and Abe, being champions of economic reforms, are deemed the architects of the current national resurgence happening in their respective countries.

Economically, the India-Japan ties have been steadily climbing an upward trajectory, after signing of Comprehensive Economic Partnership Agreement in 2011. Over 1000 Japanese companies have set up base in India, making Japan the fourth largest investor in India.

These include Sony, Toyota, Hitachi and Mitsubishi. In the last 12 years, Japanese companies have invested US$12.66 billion in India, accounting for seven per cent of total FDI inflow into India.

The Prime Minister, Shri Narendra Modi at the Business luncheon hosted by Nippon Keidanren – the Japanese Chamber of Commerce and Industry, and the Japan-India Business Cooperation Committee, in Tokyo, Japan on September 01, 2014.

During his stay in Japan, Modi visited Kyoto, the old Japanese capital, and Tokyo. He held wide ranging discussions on various issues ranging from investments in infrastructure, cooperation on bilateral and multilateral issues to security of the region.

Japan's Commitment towards Modi's 'Make in India' Initiative

Japan renewed its commitment to play an increasingly important role in India's economic transformation and development. It pledged a qualitatively new level of Japanese support and partnership for India's inclusive development, including transformation of India's manufacturing and infrastructure sectors. It announced its intention to realise ¥3.5 trillion or US$35 billion or ₹ 2,10,000 crore of public and private investments and financing to India over the next five years.

Besides economic cooperation, the two leaders decided to make their relationship comprehensive and broad-based and agreed to intensify their political dialogue and cooperation. They decided to give more thrust to defence cooperation, including collaboration in defence technology and equipment, and maritime security while expanding cooperation in advanced technology, science & technology, people to people exchanges and educational exchanges.

The two countries decided to intensify cooperation in non-proliferation, UN reforms, space security and cyber security, and in regional forums, like East Asia Summit. The two leaders described as 'significant' the progress in their negotiations on civil nuclear cooperation in recent months and the two countries now have better understanding of each other's position.

The Prime Minister, Shri Narendra Modi unveiling the plaque to inaugurate the Vivekananda Cultural Centre (Embassy of India), in Tokyo, Japan on September 02, 2014.

A new level of mutual trust and the commitment of the two countries to deepen their strategic partnership were reflected in Japan's decision to remove several Indian entities from the

Foreign End Users List, the MoU on defence exchanges and their intention to work out an agreement for collaboration on defence technologies.

The two sides reached agreements on health, roads, clean energy and women's development sectors and on Kyoto-Varanasi partnership as twin-cities.

Strategic Partnership

A document titled 'Tokyo Declaration for India-Japan Special Strategic and Global Partnership' was issued. In this, the two leaders pledged to realise the full potential of India-Japan strategic and global partnership for continuing progress and prosperity for their people and for advancing peace, stability and prosperity in Asia and the world. They described their meeting as "*the dawn of a new era in India-Japan relations*".

In their discussion on political, defence and security partnership, it was decided that they would continue the practice of annual summits and meet as often as possible on the margins of regional and multilateral meetings. The importance of the 2 plus 2 dialogue for their growing strategic partnership was acknowledged by the two leaders. This involves Foreign and Defence Secretaries of the two countries.

Emphasising on strategic partnership between the two countries, the two leaders decided to upgrade and strengthen their defence relations. This was sealed through a Memorandum of Cooperation and Exchanges for defence. Regularising bilateral maritime exercises and Japan's continued participation in India-US Malabar series of exercises was also envisaged by the two leaders.

Welcoming Japan's policy on transfer of defence equipment and technology, Modi stated that this initiative would bring about a new era of cooperation in defence equipment and technology. The subject of the progress on the Joint Working Group on cooperation in US-2 amphibian aircraft and its technology was also touched upon by the two Prime Ministers.

Highlighting the importance of maritime and cyber security, the two leaders reaffirmed their commitment of enhanced security. The two leaders were in consonance as regards the freedom of navigation and overflight, civil aviation and safety. They also agreed upon unimpeded lawful commerce and peaceful settlement of disputes in accord with international law.

Japan-India Global Partnership for Peace and Security

Acknowledging the need for a 'closer and stronger' strategic partnership between the two countries in the present-day increasing disorder, pressures and pulls in the world, the two leaders declared peace, stability and prosperity in the world, Asia, Pacific and Indian Ocean Region as indispensable for the prosperous future for the two countries.

Collaborating with other countries in the region and beyond, the two leaders held a common vision of tackling region's challenges, deepening regional cooperation and integration, strengthening regional economic and security forums and promoting peaceful resolution of disputes. The need for closer consultation and coordination in regional forums, including the East Asia Summit, was felt by the two leaders.

Condemning terrorism in all its forms, the two leaders laid emphasis on stronger international partnership by adopting the Comprehensive Convention on International Terrorism at the earliest. They felt that this will reinvigorate multilateral action and help in combating this menace.

The Prime Minister, Shri Narendra Modi shares a lighter moment with Japanese ceremonial drummers, at the inauguration of the TCS Japan Technology and Cultural Academy, in Tokyo, Japan on September 02, 2014.

Furthermore, the two leaders noted with concern the continued turmoil in the West Asia- Middle East region that is having a devastating impact on countries and people in the region. Both India and Japan have shared interests in this region in terms of energy security.

The two leaders held a common dream on the Afghan issue on making Afghanistan a *"united, independent, sovereign, stable and democratic nation free of terrorism, extremism and external interference"* through economic development and enhanced security.

The need to make UN Security Council more representative was the outcome of the third round of India-Japan consultations on UN issues held in Japan in July 2014 and was endorsed by the two leaders. To this end both wanted its comprehensive reform.

Civil Nuclear Energy

The two leaders expressed satisfaction over the progress in negotiations on the Agreement for Cooperation in the peaceful uses of nuclear energy.

Removal of six of India's space and defence-related entities from Japan's Foreign End User list by the Japanese government in the context of non-proliferation was hailed by Modi. The two leaders considered this as an impetus for enhanced trade and collaboration in high technology between the two countries. India's commitments towards non-proliferation and using its resources and technology for delivery systems for weapons of Mass Destruction, was appreciated by the Japanese Prime Minister.

PM Abe pledged total support to India for gaining full membership in the four international export control regimes, namely Nuclear Suppliers Group, Missile Technology Control Regime, Wassenaar Arrangement and Australia Group.

Partnership for Prosperity

Appreciating Modi's bold and ambitious vision, Japan assured its continuous support for India's economic development.

The India-Japan Investment Promotion Partnership envisages doubling Japan's foreign direct investment and the number of Japanese companies in India within five years.

An overseas development assistance of ¥3.5 trillion of public and private investment was promised to India by Japan for financing projects in the areas of infrastructure, connectivity, transport systems, smart cities, rejuvenation of Ganga and other rivers, manufacturing, clean energy, skill development, water security, food processing and agro industry, agricultural cold chain and rural development.

Japan is considering pledging ODA loan of ¥50 billion to IIFCL (India Infrastructure Finance Company Limited) for public-private partnership infrastructure projects in India. This prompted Modi to assure his Japanese counterpart of improvement of Indian business environment through tax, administrative and financial regulations.

Japan's interest in enhanced connectivity and development of the North East region and its linking to other economic corridors to India and to Southeast Asia was discussed by the two leaders.

Briefing PM Abe regarding his initiative for smart cities and renewal of heritage cities, including Varanasi, Modi extracted Abe's willingness to support this initiative and got the document promoting partnership city arrangement between Varanasi and Kyoto signed.

Realising Modi's eagerness for high speed railway system, PM Abe urged him to introduce Shinkansen system for the Ahmedabad-Mumbai route for which Japan would provide financial, technical and operational support. Progress on India-Japan economic partnership – the Western DFC (Dedicated Freight Corridor), DMIC (Delhi-Mumbai Industrial Corridor) and CBIC (Chennai-Bengaluru Industrial Corridor) was also discussed and the need for Japan to associate with Ahmedabad Metro Project was also projected.

The two leaders agreed for a joint strategic collaboration in global oil and natural gas market, including joint procurement of LNG, development of oil & gas and promotion of flexible LNG markets.

Collaboration in Science & Technology and Other Fields

The two countries agreed to collaborate in science & technology, innovation, education, skill development, health, information and communication technology for offering new opportunities for their skilled manpower.

Promoting life sciences, the two sides agreed to boost stem cell research, material science, cognitive science, applied mathematics, ocean technology, clean and renewable energy, water technology, climate change science and outer space.

Expressing the importance of people-to-people contact, that eventually led to richness of relationship, the two sides decided to promote tourism, youth exchanges, educational collaboration and cultural exchanges. Modi extracted Japan's support for his pet 'Digital India' initiative, as also its collaboration in healthcare and women empowerment projects.

Modi's State Visit to CHINA (May 14-16, 2015)

"Chinese development brings enormous opportunities and benefits to the Asia Pacific and the world, and the business opportunities are lasting and limitless."
– **Xi Jinping**, President of People's Republic of China

Indo-China Relations

Before Modi's State visit to China, he had his first meeting with Chinese President Xi Jinping on the sidelines of the 6th BRICS Summit at Fortaleza in Brazil on July 15, 2014. The meeting that was scheduled for 30 to 40 minutes actually lasted approximately 80 minutes, showing the importance the two leaders accorded each other.

The Prime Minister, Shri Narendra Modi visiting the Da Xing Shan Temple, in Xi'an, Shaanxi Province, China on May 14, 2015.

Their discussions were described as 'freewheeling', where both the leaders focussed on establishing personal rapport. The discussions were officially focussed on all aspects of the bilateral agenda, as well as, on regional global issues. How much importance was attached to the meeting could be gauged from President Xi's statement that "*when India and China meet, the whole world watches.*"

During the 80-minute talk, the two leaders referred to the civilisational linkages between India and China, the heritage that binds the people together.

Modi pushed forward his development agenda and emphasised on economic linkages between the two countries. He spoke about infrastructural cooperation, industrial parks and trade deficit in favour of China. President Xi agreed on the need for much more balanced approach to trade and indicated the possibilities of enhanced trade in services from India besides expansion of Indian exports and Chinese tourism to India as being areas of opportunities.

President Xi also accepted a suggestion to look into the possibilities of opening an additional route for Manasarovar Yatra to facilitate Indian pilgrims.

Modi also sought a greater role for India in SCO, where it is currently holding an observer's status.

Last, but not the least, Modi did not lose the opportunity to touch upon the sensitive boundary issue which has remained unresolved till date. It was emphasised that solution to this was important for maintaining peace and tranquillity on the border.

Modi's Visit to China

"China and India are two great and old civilisations of the world. They have provided many lights of knowledge on the entire human society. Today, we together, represent more than one third of the Global population...India and China have a common history of 5,000 years and a common boundary of over 3,400 kilometers", said Modi in Shanghai.

Modi went to China on a State Visit in May 2015 at the invitation of Chinese Prime Minister Li Keqiang where he also called on President Xi Jinping. Modi had earlier visited China as Chief Minister of Gujarat, but this was his first as Prime Minister of India. It was also intended to take forward the understanding reached between India and China during President Xi's visit to Gujarat in September 2014, which was described as a significant milestone in the development of bilateral relations between the two countries.

According to the joint statement issued after the meeting between the two Prime Ministers on May 15, 2015, the two leaders noted that India-China bilateral relations were poised to play a defining role in the 21st century, not only in Asia, but also globally. Both India and China are now emerging economic powers in the region.

The Prime Minister, Shri Narendra Modi being warmly welcomed by a girl child on his arrival at Xi'an Xiangyang International Airport, in China on May 14, 2015.

The talks between them covered wide range of issues including strengthening of political dialogue and strategic communication, closer developmental partnership, culture and people-to-people exchanges, new avenues for cooperation, trans-border cooperation and shaping of regional and global agenda. As many as 24 Memoranda of Understanding and Agreements were signed during the visit.

In addition, 26 agreements were signed at India-China Forum during Prime Minister Modi's visit to Shanghai the next day, May

16, the ground for which was laid by Modi in his keynote address to the forum.

Modi's speech was testimony to his commitment to 'Make in India' initiative and for bringing about rapid industrialisation in India.

Recalling the 5000-year-old common history between the two countries, and rich Buddhist linkages between the two great Asian powers, he said that the 21st century belongs to Asia and Buddhism will be a further unifying and catalysing force among the Asian countries.

His speech was self-explanatory of his economic agenda and how India and China work together for development of the region. Some excerpts of his speech:

"We have a lot in common and we can do a lot together. As we helped each other grow spiritually, we have to help each other grow economically. There are instances of such economic exchanges in the past...we both have potentials of growth and problems of poverty which we can tackle together. I am personally committed to take the cooperative process forward."

"We are very keen to develop the sectors where China is strong. We need your involvement. The scope and potential, the breadth and length of infrastructure and related developments is very huge in India...."

"We have planned to build 50 million houses by 2022. In addition, we are going to develop smart cities and mega industrial corridors. For this purpose we have refined our FDI Policy in construction. We are also coming up with a regulatory framework for this sector."

"We have targeted 175 Giga Watts of renewable energy in next few years. In addition, modernisation of railway systems, construction of highways, putting up new ports and modernisation

of the old ones, upgradation of existing airports and putting up regional airports to enhance connectivity were part of India's priority areas where Chinese industries have great opportunity to invest in."

"In financial services too, my Government is moving towards a more inclusive and faster delivery of financial products including bank loans and insurance. For this purpose we have opened 140 million bank accounts, increased FDI in insurance up to 49% and have set up a MUDRA (Micro Units Development and Refinance Agency) Bank to fund the micro business."

Modi praised China for its achievements in manufacturing sector and said India also wanted to promote manufacturing in a big way to create jobs for the youth who formed 65 per cent of its population.

He said, *"India's economic environment has changed. Our regulatory regime is much more transparent, responsive and stable...We do believe that FDI is important and it will not come in the country without a globally competitive business environment. Therefore, we have rationalised a number of issues which were bothering the investors."*

Among the steps taken by India are:

(i) Removal of regressive taxation regime and making it more transparent, stable and predictable;

(ii) Reduction in complicated procedures, making them available at one platform, preferably online;

(iii) Simplifying the forms and formats has been taken on war footing;

(iv) Fast approvals in industry and infrastructure, including environmental clearances, extending the industrial licences, de-licencing of defence items, and simplification of cross-border trade;

(v) Tax free bonds in the infrastructure sector including roads and railways.

These measures resulted in building up an enhanced investor confidence. As a result FDI inflows have gone up by 39 per cent during April 2014 and February 2015 against the same period in previous year. India registered a growth rate of above seven per cent.

This was perhaps the first time that an Indian Prime Minister wooed Chinese investors in this manner to invest in India, for economic development and political stability of the continents.

"You are the 'factory of the world', whereas we are the 'Back office of the world'. You give thrust on production of hardware, while India focuses on software and services," Modi observed.

Later Modi raised similar points to realise 'Make in India' mission and exhorted China for economic partnership in a big way, while speaking at the launch of India-China Forum of State Provincial Leaders at the Tsinghua University, Beijing on May 15.

Indirectly lobbying for inclusion of India as a permanent member of the UN Security Council, Modi said, "A *resurgent Asia is seeking a bigger voice in global affairs. India and China seek a greater role in the world. It may be reforms in the United Nations Security Council or the new Asian Infrastructure Investment Bank.*"

Bilateral Relations

Acknowledging the significance of President Xi's visit to India in September 2014 in development of bilateral relations, the two leaders reviewed its progress. Taking this visit as core component, the two leaders felt a historic imperative for the two countries to enrich their bilateral relations by building stronger developmental partnership.

The two leaders recognised the opportunity of realising Asian Century in the wake of both India and China reemerging as two major powers in the region and the world. They acknowledged the defining role that bilateral relations between India-China are poised to play in the 21st Century both in Asia and at a global level. Both the leaders envisaged unfolding of mutually supportive process through pursuing national developmental goals and security interests by the two countries. This entails displaying mutual respect and sensitivity to the concerns, interests and aspirations of both the nations. This would provide a new basis for pursuing state-to-state relations to strengthen the international system.

Strengthening Political Dialogue and Strategic Communication

The two leaders acknowledged strengthening of bilateral relationship between the two countries and the growing international role of India and China. This has given the impetus to the two leaders to open all lines of communications through frequent exchanges at the leadership level and by fully rejuvenating the existing dialogue mechanisms.

The two leaders not only agreed to hold regular visits of Heads of State/Government, but also acknowledged the opportunities provided by the presence of their leaders for consultations on bilateral relations and issues of regional and global importance.

The two leaders agreed to establish a State/Provincial Leaders' Forum and its first meeting, held in Beijing on May 15, 2015, saw the participation of both Modi and Premier Li.

The Prime Minister, Shri Narendra Modi at the launch of the Centre for Gandhian and Indian Studies, at Fudan University, in Shanghai, China on May 16, 2015.

The contribution of high-level exchanges organised by the Ministry of External Affairs of India and the International Department of the Central Committee of the Communist Party of China for fostering cooperation and understanding encouraged the two sides to institutionalise and expand the exchange mechanism.

It was agreed by the two leaders to establish additional Consulate General in Chengdu by India and in Chennai by China. This will facilitate and promote greater cultural, tourism and people-to-people engagement between the two countries.

The two leaders acknowledged the importance of enhanced military ties in building mutual trust and confidence between the two countries. As an outcome, India welcomed the visit of a Vice Chairman of the Central Military Commission of China to India and China invited Indian Defence Minister and other military officials to China, both in 2015. It was also decided to hold the fifth joint counter-terrorism training between the two armies in 2015. The Navies of the two countries will not only exchange visits of naval ships, but also hold PASSEX (Passing Exercise) and SAR (South Asian Region) exercises.

The two leaders acknowledged the effectiveness of the Agreements and Protocols signed between the two countries in maintaining peace and tranquillity in the border areas. Annual visits and exchanges between the two Military Headquarters and neighbouring military commands were envisaged by the two leaders to enhance border defence cooperation. The two sides would also endeavour to operationalise the hotline between the two Military Headquarters and establish meeting points at all sectors of the India-China border areas.

Boundary Issue

Terming the boundary settlement between the two countries as a strategic objective of the two governments, the two leaders sought a political settlement of the boundary question, keeping the long-term interests of the two peoples in mind. They assessed the progress made through the mechanism of the Special Representatives and shared their commitment to abide by the three-stage process of boundary settlement for an early solution that is fair, reasonable and mutually acceptable to both.

The two leaders reiterated their commitment to deal with the boundary question proactively and any difference arising out of it not be allowed to interfere in the bilateral relations of the two countries. Both the leaders recognised the importance of peace and tranquillity on the India-China border in development and continued growth of bilateral relations. Till the final resolution of the boundary question is reached, the two sides committed to continue to make efforts to maintain peace and tranquillity in the border areas.

Closer Developmental Partnership

Terming closer developmental partnership as important, the two sides resolved to work together to further strengthen it. This would not only provide impetus to economic growth and prosperity of the two countries, but also to their respective regions and the world.

The two leaders acknowledged the positive contribution of increase in two-way trade and investment flows between the two countries in the past few years in strengthening their overall bilateral relationship and supporting mutual growth and development. The two leaders decided to take the necessary measures to remove all hurdles to bilateral trade and investment and agreed to facilitate greater market access to each other. This entails supporting the local governments of the two countries to strengthen trade and investment exchanges in identified sectors in the Five Year Trade and Economic Development Plan signed in September 2014 that included Indian pharmaceuticals, Indian IT services, tourism, textiles and agro-products.

Resolving to take joint measures to alleviate the skewed bilateral trade, the two leaders decided to make full use of the India-China Joint Economic Group and agreed to uphold the spirit of mutual cooperation and reciprocity on issues of tariff reduction on relevant Indian products under the framework of Asia-Pacific Trade Agreement.

The two leaders laid emphasis on the importance of the Strategic Economic Dialogue mechanism to explore new areas of bilateral economic cooperation and decided to hold its next meeting in India during the second half of 2015. The Strategic Economic Dialogue will be co-chaired by Vice Chairman of NITI (National Institution for Transforming India) Aayog of India and Chairman of NDRC (National Development and Reform Commission) of China.

The positive momentum garnered by investment projects impressed the two leaders and India's invitation to 'Make in India' was well received by the Chinese companies. Indian companies, too, get a chance to expand their presence in China.

The two leaders noted with satisfaction the cooperation in the Railway sector that included the speed raising on Chennai-Bengaluru-Mysore line, the proposal of high speed rail link for the Delhi-Nagpur section, the redevelopment for Bhubaneswar and Baiyappanahalli stations, heavy haul transportation training and setting up of a railway university.

For building closer developmental partnership, the two leaders expressed their readiness to enhance cooperation between the financial regulators and enterprises of the two countries.

Culture and People-to-People Exchanges

Modi witnessed the Yoga-Taichi demonstration event with Premier Li that was held in Beijing on May 15, 2015. The two leaders agreed to organise events related to the International Yoga Day on 21 June 2015, while welcoming the collaboration between the Indian Council for Cultural Relations and Yunnan National University.

Terming the enhanced exchanges among education institutions of the two countries most encouraging, the two leaders were confident that this will play a positive role in socio-economic development of the two sides. The signing of the expanded Educational Exchange Programme between the two countries was welcomed by both.

The progress achieved in the India-China Cultural Exchange Initiative was endorsed by the two leaders, who committed to holding annual exchange of 200 youths from each side in the second half of 2015.

Provincial Partnership

The two leaders welcomed the agreements on establishing a provincial partnership between Karnataka and Sichuan and sister-city relationships between Aurangabad-Dunhuang, Chennai-Chongqing and Hyderabad-Qingdao.

The two leaders decided to establish 'India-China Think Tanks Forum' to facilitate closer dialogue and mutual understanding between the two countries. This Forum will alternately meet in India and China every year. Institutionalising 'High Level Media Forum', the two leaders tasked their respective ministries to convene it on an annual basis, alternately in India and China.

New Avenues for Cooperation

Welcoming the initiation and expansion of cooperation in the following fields, the two leaders directed the relevant agencies to implement the projects in a purposeful manner:

(i) Vocational training and skill development through the signing of Action Plan on the establishment of Mahatma Gandhi National Institute for Skill Development and Entrepreneurship at Gandhinagar/Ahmedabad in Gujarat;

(ii) Development of smart cities with identification of GIFT City in India and Shenzhen in China as pilot smart cities for joint demonstration projects;

(iii) Peaceful uses of outer space and nuclear energy;

(iv) Public health, medical education and traditional medicine;

(v) Signing of the 2015-2020 Space Cooperation Outline between the Indian Space Research Organisation of the Republic of India and China National Space

Administration, cooperation in the field of Satellite Remote Sensing, Space-Based meteorology, Space Science, Lunar and Deep Space Exploration, Satellite Navigation, Space Components, Piggy-back Launching Services, and education and training.

(vi) Strengthen cooperation between the law enforcing agencies of the two sides including enhancing welfare of prisoners of either countries in the prisons of the other side. Discussions on an agreement for transfer of sentenced persons.

Trans-Border Cooperation

India appreciated China's willingness to provide flood-season hydrological data and the assistance in emergency management and both sides mutually pledged to further strengthen this cooperation through the Expert-Level Mechanism.

Building mutual trust through border trade, pilgrimage and other exchanges was acknowledged by the two leaders, who agreed to further broaden this cooperation. In connection with border trade, the two sides agreed to negotiate the enhancement of traded commodities to boost border trade at Nathu La, Qiangla/Lipu-Lekh Pass and Shipki La.

Facilitating Indian pilgrims travelling on pilgrimage to Kailash Manasarover (Gang Renpoche and Mapam Yun Tso), the Indian side lauded the efforts of Ministry of Foreign Affairs and the local government of Tibet Autonomous Region of China for their support and cooperation. To further facilitate Indian pilgrims, the Chinese side agreed to open a new Yatra route through Nathu La Pass.

Both the leaders agreed to discuss the developments affecting international peace and security, as also to work together to shape the regional and global agenda. They pledged to further strengthen cooperation in multilateral forums, such as RIC (Russia, India and China), BRICS and G20. They also agreed to promote the interests of developing countries and to build a better world. The G20 Summit being hosted by China in 2016 will have India's support.

Expressing strong condemnation for terrorism in all its forms, the two leaders committed themselves to cooperate on counter-terrorism. This would entail disrupting terrorist networks and their financing, stopping cross-border movement of terrorists in accordance the UN Charter and international laws. An early conclusion of the Comprehensive Convention on International Terrorism was sought by both sides.

The Chinese leader supported India's aspiration to play a greater role in the United Nations including the Security Council, since China attaches great importance to India's status in international affairs as a large developing country.

The two sides expressed their willingness to continue cooperation under the framework of Shanghai Cooperation Organisation and China welcomed India's desire for full membership of this Organisation.

The progress made in promoting cooperation under the framework of the BCIM (Bangladesh, China, India and Myanmar) Economic Corridor was welcomed by the two sides. The two sides agreed to broaden cooperation in SAARC.

Both sides welcomed the success of the Beijing APEC (Asia-Pacific Economic Cooperation) and appreciated the role of this organisation in advancing regional economic integration and in promoting regional economic growth and prosperity. Welcoming India's desire to strengthen its link with APEC, China appreciated India's role in driving the global economic growth and its support to the openness of APEC.

The Prime Minister, Shri Narendra Modi interacting with the people at the India-China Business Forum, in Shanghai, China on May 16, 2015.

The India-China Dialogue on Arms Control and Non-Proliferation held in Beijing on April 17, 2015 was welcomed by the two sides, who noted the commonalities in their approach to global arms control and non-proliferation. Both sides agreed to continue their bilateral engagement on arms control and non-proliferation.

Terming the issue of climate change of vital importance for future generations, the two leaders underscored the importance of working together and with other countries to reach a balanced and equitable climate agreement at the forthcoming CoP 21 (Conference of Parties) to UNFCCC (United Nations Framework Convention on Climate Change) to be held in Paris in the second half of 2015. This will also help in meeting common global challenge through technology transfer, collaboration for adaptation and mitigation, and financial support.

Modi's state visit to MONGOLIA (May 17-18, 2015)

"Mongolia is a country of rich and ancient heritage, unique culture and astounding natural beauty. It is a land of free and brave, peace-loving and hard-working people."
—**Tsakhiagiin Elbegdorj**, President of Mongolia

"Today Indians and Mongolians are telling the world that the bonds of hearts and minds have the strength to overcome the barriers of distance. That bond thrives through the monks from Mongolia....", said Modi during his address to the Mongolian Parliament.

The Prime Minister, Shri Narendra Modi playing a traditional Mongolian music instrument "Yochin" at Mini Naadam Festival, in Ulaanbaatar, Mongolia on May 17, 2015.

After paying a three-day tour of China, Modi paid a two-day state visit to Mongolia on May 17 and 18 , 2015, the first by an Indian Prime Minister, during which he explored the possibilities of increasing economic cooperation to realise his 'Make in India' dream.

Despite India's minimal economic engagement with Mongolia, an excellent potential for cooperation exists in the mineral sector, since Mongolia is a mineral rich country. Its natural resources of coking coal, copper, rare earths and uranium can prove indispensable for India. Although India has a civil nuclear agreement with Mongolia that permits uranium exports to India, prospecting and mining in Mongolia needs permission of Mongolia's domestic laws. The change in these laws is awaited. Another product that India is exploring is importing Cashmere wool from Mongolia.

The Prime Minister, Shri Narendra Modi unveiling foundation stone of Atal Bihari Vajpayee Centre of Excellence in IT, Comm. & Outsourcing, in Ulaanbaatar, Mongolia on May 17, 2015.

India extends a helping hand to Mongolia in training and education sectors. Under the Indian Technical and Economic Cooperation Programme, India reserves 150 slots every year for Mongolian candidates. India also annually grants 40 scholarships to Mongolian nationals in the education sector.

Hindi films and TV serials like Mahabharata, dubbed in Mongolian, were quite popular in that country.

On very first day after his arrival, Modi first went to the Gandan Monastery where he gifted a Bodhi Tree sapling, followed by talks with Mongolian Prime Minister Chimed Saikhanbileg and signing of various agreements. The gifting of Bodhi tree sapling can be seen as a gesture to bind people of the two countries spiritually. Mongolia has sizeable population which follows Buddhism.

On the same day, Modi was accorded a rare honour of addressing the specially convened session of Mongolian Parliament. The highlights of Modi's visit to Mongolia includes laying of the foundation stone for the expansion and upgradation of Atal Bihari Vajpayee Centre for Excellence in Information and Communication Technology at Ulaanbaatar and handing over of the Bhabhatron equipment for treatment of cancer patients. Modi said that this was the first demonstration of India's cooperation in the civil nuclear sector.

Later he watched a mini Naadam festival which displayed horse riding, traditional wrestling and archery.

Addressing the Mongolian Parliament, Modi won the hearts of the Mongolians when he said, "*I bring the greetings of your 1.25 billion spiritual neighbours. There is no higher form of a relationship; no bonds more sacred than this.*" Modi drew Buddhist legacy between the two countries dating back to 2,000 years.

Modi recalled how India supported Mongolia's membership of the United Nations five decades ago and on its part, Mongolia always stood in solidarity with India, in the UN and elsewhere.

Modi spoke about his 'Make in India' campaign and the various measures taken by India to ease environment for foreign investments. India, he said, had emerged as the fastest growing economy with a growth rate of 7.5 per cent. This can also benefit Mongolia, indirectly suggesting Mongolia to *"fuel our partnership"* with rich mineral resources.

"We can seize the economic opportunities of the digital world and work together to make it more secure against growing cyber threats," he said, while enlisting possible cooperation in dairy sector, Pashmina resources and healthcare sector, including traditional medicines to improve holistic treatment.

The Prime Minister, Shri Narendra Modi and the Prime Minister of Mongolia, Mr. Chimed Saikhanbileg during the Ceremonial Welcome, at the State Palace, in Mongolia on May 17, 2015.

Modi also conveyed India's decision to provide US$1 billion Line of Credit to develop institutions, infrastructure and human resources in Mongolia.

In additions, India agreed to establish a Cyber Security Centre in Mongolia's defence and security establishment. The two countries would continue to conduct defence exercises together and signed agreements to cooperate on border security and cyber security.

At the Banquet speech, Modi described the relationship between the two countries as not just one measured on the scale of commerce or driven by competition against others, but "*a relationship of immeasurable positive energy that comes from our spiritual links and shared ideals. This form of energy has enormous power to be the force of peace, progress and prosperity in the world.*"

He said, "*Although my visit to this country was short, but it was substantive and significant. Our political understanding and commitment have become stronger. Our economic cooperation has scaled new heights and our security cooperation has expanded.*"

In a press statement Prime Minister Modi said Mongolia is an integral part of India's 'Act East' policy and the destinies of India and Mongolia were closely linked with the future of the Asia Pacific Region. The two countries could work together to advance peace, stability and prosperity in this region. The agreements that the two countries signed showed the depth of their relationship. These covered areas like economic relations, development partnership, defence and security and people to people contacts. As many as 13 agreements were signed between the two countries.

India-Mongolia Strategic Partnership

The two leaders termed Modi's first visit to Mongolia as significant in the backdrop of the 60th anniversary of diplomatic relations between the two countries.

Both sides expressed satisfaction over the continued development in bilateral relations based on deep civilisational, historical, spiritual and cultural linkages, common democratic traditions and shared desire for regional and international peace and stability. Modi and Saikhanbileg decided to further consolidate this comprehensive partnership. They said that the strategic partnership between them was guided by the principles of sovereign equality of states, the principles of the United Nations Charter, collective interests of their peoples and the fundamental ideal of the Treaty of Friendly Relations and Cooperation signed by the two countries on February 22, 1994.

The two leaders expressed their support for the security architecture in the Asia Pacific region based on international law that has legitimate interests of all states of the region in its ambit.

Modi got Mongolian support for India's claim for permanent membership of the UN Security Council and Mongolia agreed with India over the need for reforms of the United Nations to make it more representative. The two leaders also pledged their reciprocal support for a non-permanent seat in the UNSC for the terms 2021-2022 and 2023-2024 respectively.

India also assured its support to Mongolia's candidacy to the UN Human Rights Council for the terms 2016-2018.

On terrorism issue, the two Prime Ministers agreed to work together for the adoption of the Comprehensive Convention on International Terrorism.

Defence and Security Cooperation was another area in which both sides agreed to continue to work towards intensifying bilateral relations.

The two Prime Ministers also pledged their full support in investment, economic cooperation and development of trade that is both equal and mutually beneficial. India will support Mongolia's endeavor to create a business friendly foreign investment regime and Mongolia would enable Indian companies to explore cooperation opportunities in the country in mining sector to a greater extent through joint venture and investment.

The Prime Minister, Shri Narendra Modi visiting the Gandan Monastery, in Mongolia on May 17, 2015.

Besides, both the countries also decided to intensify cooperation in civil nuclear domain, agriculture sector, health sector, people to people contact, education and ease travel between the two countries.

To rediscover the shared cultural heritage, both the Prime Ministers agreed to initiate a joint translation of 'Holy Tripitaka' into Mongolian language and later witnessed signing of agreements on:

(i) Air Services;
(ii) Treaty on the transfer of sentenced persons;
(iii) Cooperation in the field of animal health and dairy;
(iv) Cooperation in the field of traditional systems of medicine and Homoeopathy;
(v) Establishment of Cyber Security Training Centre in the Mongolian Defence Ministry;
(vi) Establishment of India-Mongolia Joint Friendship School in Mongolia;
(vii) Cooperation in the field of culture for the years 2015-2018;
(viii) MoU for cooperation between National Security Councils of both the countries;
(ix) MoU on renewable energy;
(x) MoU for cooperation between India's Ministry of External Affairs and Mongolian Foreign office;
(xi) MoU on cooperation in border guarding, policing and surveillance; and
(xii) MoU between Tata Memorial Centre and National Cancer Center of Mongolia for gifting of Bhabhatron-II Tele-Therapy Unit along with a radiotherapy simulator.

Modi's State Visit to SOUTH KOREA (May 18-19, 2015)

"We must give a bigger push for innovations, including in business structure, so that we can lead industry trends."
—**Lee Kum-hee**

South Korea was the last of the three East Asian countries visited by Modi after paying state visits to China and Mongolia. Soon after his arrival in Seoul on May 18, Modi visited the National Cemetery and paid his tributes. Thereafter he attended a big reception organised in his honour by the Indian community.

The Prime Minister, Shri Narendra Modi and the President of Republic of Korea, Ms. Park Geun-hye, at the delegation Level Talks between India and South Korea, in Seoul, South Korea on May 18, 2015.

This was all before the official welcome ceremony which was followed by official bilateral talks between the two countries and signing of agreements. In the evening he attended the banquet dinner hosted by South Korean President Park Geun-hye in his honour.

Modi participated in the 6th Asian Leadership Conference, visited Cheonggyecheon Stream, attended India-Republic of Korea CEOs Forum meeting, interacted with Friends of India in South Korea and visited Hyundai Heavy Industries shipyard the next day, May 19.

Background of Indo-Korean Relations

Political and economic relations between India and Republic of Korea are described as multidimensional, based on mutual goodwill and convergence of interests.

There have been several high level visits by dignitaries of both the countries. Notable among them was that of former Prime Minister Dr. Manmohan Singh, who paid an official visit to Seoul from March 24 to 27, in 2012. This was his second visit to this country, earlier being in 2010 for the G-20 Summit. South Korean former President Lee Myung-bak's had paid a state visit to India in 2010 when he was made the chief guest at the Republic Day Celebrations in New Delhi. The meetings between the two leaders led to the deepening of bilateral strategic partnership that was forged during former President Lee Myung-bak's State visit to India.

Other top Indian dignitaries who visited South Korea included former Indian Presidents Pratibha Patil in 2011 and Dr. APJ Abdul Kalam in 2006. During President Patil's visit, the two countries signed the significant Civil Nuclear Energy Cooperation Agreement.

Bilateral trade between the two countries has been quite significant. In 2011 it crossed US$20.5 billion registering a 70 per cent growth over a two-year period. A revised trade target of US$40 billion by 2015 was established by Dr. Singh and President Lee at their meeting in Seoul on March 25, 2012.

Since antiquity, the peoples of both India and South Korea had maintained historical and cultural contacts between themselves. A 13th century historical record enshrined in a treatise called 'SamgukYusa' (*The Heritage History of the Three Kingdoms*) speaks of an Indian Princess from Ayodhya (Suriratna), who visited Korea in the year 48 AD and married King Kim-Suro, to become Queen Hur Hwang-ok. Her lineage can be traced to former President Lee's wife, Kim Yoon-ok, former President Kim Dae-jung, former President Kim Young-sam and former PM Kim Jong-pil.

The Prime Minister, Shri Narendra Modi at the Wreath Laying Ceremony, in Seoul National Cemetery, South Korea on May 18, 2015.

Like in India, in South Korea too, the enduring philosophy of the Buddha has influenced the lives and thoughts of the people of the two countries. This provides a strong link between the peoples of the two nations.

India and the Republic of Korea established consular relations in 1962. In 1973, relations were upgraded to Ambassador-level. In the post-cold war era, South Korean popular quest for democracy, which was introduced in 1987, created a natural affinity between the countries. In the course of time, South Korea's open market policies found resonance with India's economic liberalisation and 'Look East' policy.

Major Korean conglomerates (Chaebols), such as Samsung, Hyundai Motors and LG have made significant investments into India, estimated at US$2.6 billion, till September 2012. Indian investments in South Korea have already exceeded US$1 billion. Novelis, a Hindalco subsidiary, acquired a Korean aluminium company by investing about US$600 million. Mahindra & Mahindra acquired a majority stake in SsangYong Motors, the country's 4th largest auto manufacturer, in March 2011, with an investment of about US$470 million. Tata Motors acquired Daewoo Commercial Vehicle Company for US$102 million in March 2004.

The two countries have excellent cultural ties, people to people contacts and good air connectivity. Indian Community in South Korea is estimated at 7500, which includes businessmen, IT professionals, scientists, research fellows, students and workers. There are about 150 businessmen dealing mainly in textiles and gems and jewellery.

Modi's 'Make in India' Initiative in South Korea

"South Korea is an indispensable partner in 'Act East' strategy, for this country's contribution to bringing peace, stability and security in the Asia Pacific Region", said Modi.

The Prime Minister, Shri Narendra Modi interacting with the people of Indian Community, at the Hyundai Heavy Industries Shipyard, in Ulsan, South Korea on May 19, 2015.

The visit of Prime Minister Modi to South Korea was part of his 'Act East' policy. Even though South Korea has a big presence in India in trade, Modi foresaw an excellent opportunity for collaborations in various fields between the two Asian countries in the direction of his initiative.

Eventually the two sides signed agreements/MoUs for avoidance of double taxation and prevention of fiscal evasion; cooperation in audio-visual co-production; cooperation between India's National Security Council Secretariat and Korea's Office of the National Security; MoU on cooperation in the field of electric power development and new energy industries and cooperation in youth matters.

Joint Statement on Special Strategic Partnership

Joint Statement on special Strategic Partnership, issued after the meeting between Prime Minister Modi and South Korean President Park Geun-hye, described the discussion between them as substantive in areas of mutual interest. They welcomed the rapid expansion and diversification of bilateral ties in recent years. They agreed to upgrade the bilateral relations to a 'Special Strategic Partnership'.

Recalling the historical and cultural bonds that connect the two peoples, the two sides resolved to boost cooperation in a wide range of areas that included foreign affairs, defense, trade and investment, science & technology, culture and people-to-people exchanges. This regional cooperation will take the bilateral relations – both political and security – to a higher level.

Modi said South Korea was an indispensable partner in its 'Act East' strategy, recognising this country's contribution to bringing peace, stability and security in the Asia Pacific Region and President Park informed him about her country's NAPCI (Northeast Asia Peace and Cooperation Initiative). The two leaders agreed to work together to find complementarities between 'Act East' policy and NAPCI to achieve shared goals.

The two countries decided to further intensify bilateral high-level exchanges, particularly in defence and security sector, which has large potential to grow.

The two sides agreed to substantiate the Special Strategic Partnership by:

(i) Establishing annual summit meetings in either country or on the margins of plurilateral events;

(ii) Holding annual Joint Commissions under the aegis of the two foreign ministers;

(iii) Strengthening democratic institutions in the respective regions by facilitating greater parliamentary exchanges;

(iv) Making partnerships between the two countries stronger by strengthening Indian and Korean institutions of defense education that include Indian National Defence College and Korean National Defense University;

(v) Holding regular consultations between the National Security Council of the two countries to strengthen cooperation in security, defense and cyber related issues;

(vi) Establishing joint Vice-Ministerial level defence and foreign affairs dialogue in the '2 plus 2' Format;

(vii) Encouraging greater cooperation between the shipyards of the two countries for defence needs;

(viii) Working towards strengthening defence cooperation through staff level talks between the navies of the two countries and holding regular exchange visits between the two armed forces;

(ix) Cooperating in cyber security to remain prepared and ward off transnational cyber threats;

(x) Participating in an appropriate degree in the area of UN Peacekeeping; and

(xi) Holding an annual track 1.5 dialogue between Korean Institute of Foreign Affairs and National Security and ICWA (Indian Council of World Affairs).

President Park praised Modi's 'Make in India' initiative for it provides new avenues to enrich and add substance to the bilateral relations. Modi invited South Korea to be a privileged partner in this initiative, highlighting enormous potential for further development.

Both the leaders called upon the Indian and Korean business communities to tap the huge synergies between their economies for mutual prosperity. The signing of the revised Double Taxation Avoidance Agreement was welcomed by the two.

Korean Finance for Priority Sectors

For mutual cooperation in infrastructure, the Ministry of Strategy and Finance and the Export-Import Bank of Korea expressed their intention to provide US$10 billion, comprising Economic Development Fund (US$1 billion) and export credits (US$9 billion). This would give a fillip to priority sectors, including smart cities, railways, power generation and transmission and, yet to be agreed, other sectors. The roadmap to chalk out the envisioned financial support for priority sectors will be discussed by the two Governments and the EXIM (Export-Import) Banks;

It was decided that negotiations would be held to amend the India-Korea CEPA (Comprehensive Economic Partnership Agreement) by June 2016 for achieving qualitative and quantitative increase of trade through an agreed roadmap;

Notable among other decisions were cooperation in building smart cities, steel sector, shipbuilding including construction of Indian vessels such as LNG carriers, maritime transport, possible joint business project in the area of shipping and logistics, and promotion of employment of both countries' seafarers, improved procedures for mutual export of fresh fruits and horticultural products, establishment of Korean Industrial Parks like the one in Rajasthan for helping small and medium enterprises to benefit from 'Make in India' initiative, and the decision to set up an India-Korea Joint Working Group to enhance cooperation and facilitate business collaboration through joint ventures in the field of electronic hardware manufacturing.

To enhance people-to-people contact, vital for further strengthening bilateral relations, it was decided that the civil aviation authorities of both the countries would amend the bilateral Air Services Agreement to increase connectivity and cover more cities.

Lauding Prime Minister's 'Swachh Bharat Abhiyan' to transform India, Korean President Park said that her country could make a substantial contribution to accomplish this, citing

Korea's successful rural development initiative in the 1970s. The two sides decided to promote cooperation in this regard.

India and Korea agreed to enhance exchanges between their respective ministries and agencies to bolster the integral link between economic growth, preservation of environment and clean energy.

Modi lauded the Korean Green Economy initiative and expressed India's willingness to work with Korea for mutually beneficial partnerships in deploying innovative policies and technologies to improve urban water and air quality and to protect natural resources.

The two sides welcomed the agreement between Indian Space Research Organisation and the Korea Aerospace Research Institute that will facilitate cooperation in the fields of lunar exploration, satellite navigation, space science and applications that include:

(i) Deep space cross tracking and communication support for Korean and Indian deep missions;

(ii) Sharing of data of lunar surface and radiation data collected by Chandrayan-1;

(iii) Collaboration in GAGAN-KASS interoperability and sharing experience in GAGAN (GPS Aided Geo Augmented Navigation system) and KASS (Korea Augmentation Satellite System);

(iv) Technical cooperation in the field of space science and application, satellite launch and other areas;

(v) Holding working-level talks regularly between ISRO and KARI to strengthen the cooperation in these areas.

Regarding promotion of culture, education and people-to-people exchanges, both leaders agreed to encourage the establishment of twin city and twin province/state relationships to deepen and broaden such exchanges. It was one of Modi's suggestions which immediately got Korea's recognition. Besides the two leaders decided to hold each other's national festivals in their respective countries.

The two leaders underlined the need for peace and stability on the Korean peninsula and expressed concern over the development of North Korea's nuclear weapons and ballistic missile programmes which is in violation of international obligations and commitments. They urged North Korea to comply with such norms and UN Security Council resolutions.

Terrorism was another issue on which the two leaders expressed concern and resolved to jointly work to eliminate this menace. They also called for early conclusion of negotiations on the Comprehensive Convention on International Terrorism.

PM Modi's Statement at India-Korea CEOs Forum in Seoul

Pursuing his 'Make in India' campaign, Prime Minister Modi drew historical linkages between the two countries and said he was there to further build that relationship. He said he was always fascinated by Korea for its economic development, even though it was of the size of Gujarat.

"I admire entrepreneurship of Korean people. I admire the way in which they have created and sustained their global brands. From IT and electronics to automobiles and steel Korea has given exemplary products to the world."

"We in India want to achieve a lot of what Korea has already done. That is why, I along with a large business delegation, am here."

Modi said several hundred Korean companies were operating in India and their products, particularly in consumer electronics were now household choices for Indians. *"However there is still a lot of scope for improvement....I can tell you that India was and is a land of potentials."*

The Prime Minister, Shri Narendra Modi visiting the Hyundai Heavy Industries Shipyard, in Ulsan, South Korea on May 19, 2015. The Chairman, Hyundai Heavy Industries, Mr. Choi Kil-seon is also seen.

"Now, India is also a land of enabling policy environment. There is a potential for cooperation between India's software and Korea's hardware industry. Therefore we can work together in a big way", he said, inviting South Korea to push further investments which ranks 14th in FDI inflows in India.

The Prime Minister said that ever since his government had taken over, there had been a consistent effort to create conditions for faster and inclusive growth. *"We want to make a quantum jump. The sectors which are strong in Korea are very important for the development of India."*

"Now there is a changed environment for investments and Korea can explore to invest in sectors like water, transportation, railways, sea ports, ship building, electricity including renewable, IT, infrastructure and services, electronics and construction industry."

"We have planned to build 50 million houses by 2022, develop smart cities, long industrial corridors and mega investment region. For this purpose, we have redefined our FDI policy in construction," he told the business community.

"'Make in India' initiative and Digital India initiative", Modi said, *"have been launched to promote manufacturing in a big way and create jobs for our youth and speed up development."*

"Similarly another mission 'Skill India' has also been launched in the country to create employment and promote self-employment. India had already resolved many taxation issues affecting the foreign investors. As a result, FDI inflows had gone up by 39% between April 2014 and February 2015 against the same period the previous year. India's growth rate was above seven per cent. All these provide congenial and healthy atmosphere for foreign investors", Modi told the South Korean CEOs Forum.

CHAPTER 3

'LINK WEST' POLICY

Modi's Visits to US, France, Germany and Canada

US and Modi: A New Beginning

"Change will not come if we wait for some other person or some other time. We are the ones we've been waiting for. We are the change that we seek." —**Barack Obama**

Modi's Vision Statement for the US-India Strategic Partnership read, "*chalein saath saath*" (together we move forward). "*As leaders of two great democratic nations with diverse traditions and faiths, we share a vision for a partnership in which the United States and India work together, not just for the benefit of both our nations, but for the benefit of the world.*"

"*The currents of kinship and commerce, scholarship and science tie our countries together. They allow us to rise above differences by maintaining the long-term perspective. Every day, in myriad ways, our cooperation fortifies a relationship that matches the innumerable ties between our peoples, who have produced works of art and music, invented cutting-edge technology and responded to crises across the globe.*"

Armed with the twin mantras – fast track diplomacy and smart development – Modi went to the United States. Modi set his compass towards the West after engaging himself with leaders of the SAARC countries and extended neighbours, China and

Japan. The US is India's largest trading partner and is fifth largest source of foreign investments into India.

It was Modi's maiden voyage to the super power, where he spent five days. Among other engagements in the US, he had one-on-one meeting with President Barack Obama; attended a huge reception hosted by the Indian diaspora at the Madison Square Garden, the venue better known for celebrity rock stars and singers; addressed the United Nations General Assembly; and held informal meeting with UN Secretary-General Ban-Ki-moon. Modi became the first foreign leader to have been accorded such an honour and the event was beamed live on giant screens at the Times Square, the heart of Manhattan visited by thousands every day.

The Prime Minister, Shri Narendra Modi addressing the 69th Session of the United Nations General Assembly, in New York on September 27, 2014.

Modi at UNO

Delivering his maiden speech in the 69th session of the UN General Assembly on September 27, 2014, in New York, Modi called for reforms and expansion of UN Security Council, including India's long-standing demand of a permanent membership. He expressed his concerns over the relevance of a 20th century set up in 21st century and stressed the need to evaluate UN's performance of the past 70 years.

The Prime Minister argued why UN should serve as G-All for global governance instead of several parallel sub-groupings like G7 and G20.

Terrorism

Expressing India's concern over terrorism of which India had been a victim for decades, he urged for immediate implementation of comprehensive policy on international terrorism by the UN. He offered a pro-active role in it.

Citing India's unwavering commitment to multilateral processes to advance peace and security and promote broad-based inclusive economic development in the world, Modi said India's contribution to UN peacekeeping operations over decades was a strong testimony of its efforts to contribute to the achievement of the objectives of the UN charter.

Prior to his address to the UNGA (United Nations General Assembly), Modi, along with External Affairs Minister Sushma Swaraj, met UN Secretary General Ban-Ki-moon and discussed UN governance and related issues.

International Yoga Day

After making a brief comment on climate change and clean energy, Modi emphasised the importance of incorporating Yoga in modern day lifestyle and urged the world leaders and the UN officials to observe an International Yoga Day. Modi feasted on a dinner hosted in his honour at the White House.

Soon after his arrival in New York, the Indian Prime Minister interacted with the Mayor of New York, Bill de Blasio and met Nobel Laureate for Medicine, Prof Harold Varmus.

The Prime Minister, Shri Narendra Modi and the Union Minister for External Affairs and Overseas Indian Affairs, Smt. Sushma Swaraj meeting the former US President, Mr. Bill Clinton and former US Secretary of State, Mrs. Hillary Clinton, in New York on September 29, 2014.

Quality of Life

Keen on improving and rejuvenating the quality of life in India, Modi discussed with New York Mayor, Bill de Blasio the steps he was taking to improve the quality of life in New York. Public housing was one such subject of discussion and Modi was informed that New York would be building something like half a million houses over a ten-year period. On policing, Modi enquired about strengthening of New York police force after the 9/11 attacks. There were also detailed discussions on common threats faced by big cities in terms of terror threats. Modi sought suggestions from New York City authorities on handling large crowds in context of the Indian massive Kumbha Mela.

Public Health

Modi discussed cancer and public health with Prof. Varmus, Director of NCI (National Cancer Institute) in New York, who had his internship at Bareilly, India in the 60s. In the half-hour discussion both stressed the need for greater partnership between developed institutes on research matters, public health issues, diabetes, obesity and their impact on cancer. Modi's interaction with the professor displayed his concern for the public health in India.

After his address at Madison Square Garden to the Indian Diaspora, Modi met Congresswoman Tulsi Gabbard, a representative of Hawaii, and the Israeli Prime Minister, Benjamin Netanyahu.

Gabbard largely conveyed her own interest in India and yoga. She is the first Hindu Congresswoman in the US and expressed her interest in Vedic scriptures. She also discussed her approach towards issues on defence and international cooperation, in terms of working against common threats in the shape of terrorism. The meeting lasted half-an-hour.

The meeting with Israeli Prime Minister, Benjamin Netanyahu, was more substantive. Economic ties between India and Israel are growing rapidly and India's trade with Israel is pegged at US$6 billion. The areas of discussion related to agriculture and water management, in both of which Israel possesses great expertise.

Modi invited Israel to work with India in urban development and added that India had about 500 cities, where water management was a major issue. Modi sought to know from Israel its views on developments in West Asia. Explaining his views on the matter at length, the Israeli Prime Minister invited Modi to visit his country.

Next day, on the sidelines of the UNGA, Modi held a number of bilateral meetings that included several leaders – Sri Lankan President Rajapaksa, Bangladesh Prime Minister Sheikh Hasina and Nepalese Prime Minister Sushil Koirala – who praised and fully supported Modi's proposal of holding an International Yoga Day.

The various leaders discussed issues of mutual interests with Modi. While Bangladesh PM Hasina raised the issues of Teesta and the land boundary, Nepalese PM Koirala reminded him of his promise of visiting Janakpur and Lumbini during his next visit to Nepal for the SAARC Summit. The two leaders wanted an early date for his visit to their respective countries. This showed Modi's personal rapport with these leaders.

Modi hosted a meeting over breakfast with the Chief Executive Officers of largely Fortune 500 companies, where he laid out his vision for economic development and 'Make in India' campaign. The very purpose of this meeting was to attract investments for India. This was part of his attempt on the one hand to brainstorm and get ideas and on the other to hard sell and promote his vision of India and inclusive development.

He told them, "*India is open-minded and we want change, and we want change that is not one-sided. And for that change we want inputs and investments from a variety of sources, not only citizens, but also industrialists and investors.*"

Modi laid out what he had done in the past three to four months and what he intended to achieve under the 'Make in India' initiative. He informed the gathering that India has opened up investments in certain areas, like the Railways (100 per cent) and defence (49 per cent) and sought their responses, which were positive on the whole.

The Prime Minister, Shri Narendra Modi paying tribute to Mahatma Gandhi, at Washington DC on September 30, 2014.

He allayed the fear expressed by some CEOs regarding the tax regime and assured them of his commitment to a stable tax regime. Similar apprehensions were also expressed on current policies and the environment.

About their concerns over the allocation of coal blocks required by the energy sector, the Prime Minister clarified that he wanted to convert the judgment of the Supreme Court on coal allocations into a major opportunity to move forward and clean up the past. He accorded highest priority to energy requirements and assured them of quick decisions from his government.

The Black Rock Corporation, meanwhile, agreed to have a major investor conference in India early next year, where they would work with the Indian Government to bring in major investors from all across the globe. The corporation said it was confident to have investment opportunities worth US$6 billion in a few months.

After the breakfast interactions with the CEOs, Modi met former US President Bill Clinton and his wife, former Secretary of State, Hillary Clinton and discussed the initiatives of Clinton Foundation in India. The Prime Minister spoke about the efforts being made to clean up River Ganga and requested the Foundation to consider working on small areas in this endeavour. Bill Clinton described the project as "*sacred and a smart approach.*" Senator Clinton added that this effort would send a message to other countries in Asia and "*set the tone for a renaissance in terms of addressing in Asia how people interact with water bodies.*"

Modi-Obama Meeting

In the evening, Prime Minister Modi and President Obama met over dinner and the official spokesman described the discussions as "*largely a sort of a get-to-know-each-other approach.*"

There were commonalities in the approach of both the leaders on technology and e-governance initiatives.

During the 90-minute deliberations, Modi reiterated his 'Make in India' plan, his development vision and how he felt that the United States could help out in this vision.

The President Barack Obama of the United States welcomes the Prime Minister, Shri Narendra Modi, at the dinner hosted in his honour, at the White House, in Washington DC on September 30, 2014.

The two leaders continued their deliberations the next morning in restricted format as well as in delegation-level talks, when they met at the White House. Considering the goodwill prevailing between the two countries, both Modi and Obama felt that they should try and focus on some big things that they can achieve in a finite time period during the next few years. It was therefore incumbent on both to work towards strengthening and deepening the new relationship between the two countries.

Of the nearly two hours meeting, 90 minutes were devoted to the delegation-level talks and about 20 minutes for Modi and Obama's interactions. Conversations were held in the spirit of what the two countries could do together.

There was a great deal of understanding of the interest and challenges that India is facing in its developmental path and a great deal of interest in the United States in ways in which it can helpfully partner India in meeting its developmental objectives, like the inclusive economic development, development of infrastructure and urban infrastructure, defence and security and people to people interaction.

Besides nuclear issue, the two leaders focussed on areas of mutual interests, business collaborations, investment in new environment offered by India through its 'Make in India' campaign, construction of smart cities and infrastructure.

On infrastructure, economics and trade matters, the US agreed to be the lead partner in developing three smart cities or upgrading them as three smart cities – Allahabad, Ajmer and Visakhapatnam. In these, the US firms would be the lead partners.

Besides, it was also decided that a partnership platform would be established with USAID (United States Agency for International Development), business and civil society, such as the Gates Foundation for Indian Municipal, State and Union entities to leverage private capacity for upgradation of water, sanitation and sewage in 500 cities to facilitate access to clean water and sanitation. It was named as 'WASH (Clean Water, Sanitation and Hygiene for All) Alliance'.

In addition, it was decided to form an Indian-US Investment Initiative for serving as a clearing platform for all infrastructure investments from the United States and India.

In line with Modi's 'Make in India' initiative, a manufacturing extension partnership will be formed which would enable the US National Institute of Standards and Technology to help small and medium enterprises in India build business plans, raise themselves to global standards, and to improve manufacturing capacity.

On strategic partnership, the US President affirmed that India meets the requirements for MTCR (Missile Technology Control Regime) and is ready for membership in the Nuclear Suppliers Group. He assured that the US was creating an interagency contact group to address all implementation issues to speed up the deployment of US-origin nuclear reactors in India.

To speed up the civil nuclear partnership, an interagency working group had been created to deal with all issues including liability and administrative, technological and techno-commercial issues. Besides it was also decided to renew the framework agreement for India-US defence cooperation for a further period of 10 years.

On defence, trade and technology initiative between the two countries, it was decided to try and identify unique and transformative technologies products, which will then be tied up in the next few months. A Special Task Force was being set up for the purpose.

US Support for India's UNSC Permanent Membership

Modi's lobbying for India's permanent seat in UNSC (United Nations Security Council) also got the US seal. The US reaffirmed its support for it and to enhance India's voice and vote in international financial institutions.

Agreeing to expand trilateral partnerships in Afghanistan and among African partners, it was decided that the US and India would work together in areas such as food security, agricultural training and women's empowerment.

Indo-US Partnership in Various Sectors

Both US and India agreed to enhance partnerships in sectors like education, IT, skill development, health and exchange of youth delegations to promote people-to-people contact. Agreement on a partnership to bring global standards to skill development in India through a nationwide certification system is in line with PM Modi's effort to ensure that skilling is done at high speed and at global standards, so that Indian youth is able to meet the opportunities and job challenges all over the world.

Agreeing on a knowledge partnership for a new IIT (Indian Institute of Technology) to be set up in India, it was decided to set up a new platform called GIAN (Global Initiative for Academic Networks) to establish mechanisms to bring up to 1000 teachers a year from the top 100 US universities to teach in the Indian central universities. This would create openings for greater flow of academics on both sides.

Addressing India's energy concerns, the US agreed on a billion-dollar concessional financing from EXIM for India's Renewable Energy Development Agency for rapid expansion of solar energy projects in India. Besides, the US also agreed to upgrade national institutes of wind, solar and bio-energy in India to world standards. Similar cooperation was assured in creating new energy innovation laboratories in India.

On the environmental side, the two countries would work for air quality through their respective agencies.

Digital India Project

Among other issues which got full support from the US was Prime Minister Modi's pet 'Digital India' project, which included digital infrastructure for e-governance and for e-services, and the collaborations in Space. The two countries decided to set up a joint working group on Mars exploration with the intention of partnering a Mars mission together.

To sum up, Modi's visit to US was a success. His 'charisma' swayed the US to acknowledge his vision of 'Make in India' campaign.

Modi & European Union Countries

Modi's State visit of three European countries commenced in April 2015. He was in France on April 9 to 11, in Germany from April 12 to 14 and in Canada from April 14 to 17.

Modi in FRANCE (April 9-11, 2015)

"Deliberation is the work of many men; action, of one alone." —**Charles de Gaulle**

France is an important country with which it enjoys growing cooperation in strategic sectors, especially in defence, space, civil nuclear and security sectors. The two countries also have expanding trade and investment ties, cooperation in science &

technology and increasing exchanges in cultural, educational and tourism sectors.

India and France are strategic partners, and consult and support each other on international matters. Their mutual understanding and commitment benefit the international community at large and the two tackle global challenges through joint efforts, even while maintaining their independence and strategic autonomy.

India enjoys full backing of France in its claim for a permanent membership of the UN Security Council and shares Indian view of reforming the United Nations to make it more representative in the modern day. The two countries are in sync as regards their concerns and objectives regarding non-proliferation of weapons of mass destruction. India's accession to the multilateral export control regimes, namely, NSG (Nuclear Suppliers Group), MTCR, the Australia Group and the Wassenaar Arrangements are supported by France, who continues to work jointly with India towards achieving it.

The Prime Minister, Shri Narendra Modi and the President of France, Mr. Francois Hollande, during the boat ride on La Seine, in Paris on April 10, 2015.

At the meeting between Modi and French President Francois Hollande, discussions were held on issues ranging from climate change, security, defence, space, nuclear energy, economic cooperation, cooperation in the field of heritage and culture, people-to-people contact and cooperation in the field of education, science and technology, sports and health in addition to development of smart cities, an important initiative of the Modi government.

Climate Change

Both countries were on the same page and pledged to work together regarding the issue of climate and deemed it vital for the world and future generations. To this end, Modi assured unstinted support to France for success in CoP 21 to UNFCCC, to be held in Paris. The importance of working together and with other countries to arrive at the ambitious, comprehensive, and equitable climate agreement in Paris was not lost on the two leaders. They were certain that this would help in meeting this common global challenge by encouraging genuine technology collaboration for adoption and mitigation, and for financial support.

Development of Smart Cities

The French President appreciated Modi's initiative for development of smart cities as a key area to foster sustainable development solutions and showed his country's willingness to be a partner in it. He said France was ready to implement its best technological solution and share its experience in the field of integrated sustainable cities, particularly in urban planning, urban grids, water and sanitation, sustainable mobility and digital technologies.

The two leaders also agreed to include 'transport' and 'heritage' in the existing India-France Agreement for Cooperation in Sustainable Urban development.

France's interest in development of smart cities prompted India to include Smart City cooperation as an area of technical cooperation under the October 2012 MoU between France and India.

Security and Terrorism

India had witnessed terrorist attacks in the past. Recently, France also witnessed some incidents of terrorism. Therefore the two leaders expressed their concern over the menace and decided to support each other to combat this scourge. The two leaders called for steps to counter this threat by dismantling terrorist infrastructure, denying safe havens to them, bringing to justice the perpetrators and conspirators of such crimes and for strengthening international framework to forge closer cooperation in this area, including UN initiative as the draft Comprehensive Convention on International Terrorism.

The Prime Minister, Shri Narendra Modi and the President of France, Mr. Francois Hollande at the release of the stamp commemorating 50 years of Indo-French Space Cooperation, in Paris on April 10, 2015.

Both countries pledged to increase their cooperation on Counter Terrorism within the framework of Joint Working Group, and address the growing phenomenon of radicalisation.

The discussions between the two leaders also included holding bilateral dialogues to discuss ways of enhancing cooperation in the maritime domain, in particular in the Indian Ocean Region. France's closer engagement in the Indian Ocean Rim Association was welcomed by Modi.

Defence

The two leaders called to intensify cooperation not only in joint military exercises between the two countries, but also in defence technologies, and research & development. Co-developing and co-production of defence equipment in India, including transfer of know-how and technologies was also envisaged by the two leaders.

Rafale Deal

Stating India's urgent need for multi-role combat aircraft Modi expressed his intent to acquire 36 Rafale jets in fly-away condition as quickly as possible. The inter-governmental Agreement for supply of the aircraft was agreed upon and further terms will be worked out by Dassault Aviation as a separate process. There needs to be a definite time frame for delivery of the aircraft. By this initiative, Modi conveyed how much importance he gives to security and upgradation of defence forces.

Nuclear Energy and Jaitapur Nuclear Plant

An MoU was signed in 2009 between NPCIL (Nuclear Power Corporation of India Limited) and Areva for the construction of six 1650 MW nuclear power plants at Jaitapur. Modi stressed the need for early conclusion of techno-commercial discussions on project viability at the earliest.

Economic Cooperation

Modi promoted his 'Make in India' initiative by impressing upon the French President the creation of a wide range of new opportunities for French investment as an outcome of current global trends and rapid socio-economic changes in India. The environment is conducive for the French and Indian people to work together and boosting economic ties. The two leaders agreed to give impetus to both Indian and French business and industry to further increase bilateral trade and investments between the two countries. Both the leaders were of the view that the India-France CEOs Forum could play an important role in furthering business to business contacts and they welcomed the Forum's report after their meeting on April 9 and 10.

The Prime Minister, Shri Narendra Modi at the Round Table Meeting with the French CEOs on Infrastructure, in Paris on April 10, 2015.

Cooperation in the field of transport was sought by both the leaders which included modernisation of Railways, high speed and semi-high speed rail projects, urban transportation and roads in its ambit. A study by SNCF (French National Railways) made under agreement with the Indian Railways regarding upgradation of the Delhi-Chandigarh line to 200 kmph and for redevelopment of Ambala and Ludhiana Railway station also came up for discussion between the two leaders. Both lauded the successful completion of a business development study for the Mumbai-Ahmedabad high speed corridor.

Energy

Modi expressed his happiness for France's target of developing 8 to 10 GW of solar energy in India by 2020-2022 and also for French support for other renewable energy sources such as wind, biomass and hydropower. India also welcomed French AFD (Agence Française de Développement) credit line of €1 billion over the next three years for sustainable infrastructure and urban development.

Arrangement between ministries of both the countries on renewable energy cooperation included extension of credit facility by AFD for India's EESL (Energy Efficiency Services Limited) and promoting use of LED (Light Emitting Diode) lighting in select Indian municipalities.

According high priority to promoting exchanges among various states of India and Regions of France in the area of sustainable, rural and urban development through twinning arrangements and visits of business delegations was also agreed to by the two leaders.

People-to-People Contact

A Letter of Intent was signed on promoting tourism between France and India that shows immense potential for both the countries. A mutual exchange of facilities was agreed to by the two leaders. India would extend Tourist visa on Arrival – Electronic Travel Authorisation scheme to France and France would expedite issue of visa for Indian tourists to within 48 hours.

Heritage/Cultural Cooperation

A range of initiatives undertaken by Indian and French institutions to promote and preserve the unique heritage of the two countries was welcomed by the two leaders, who noted the successful organisation of two editions of the Festival of France in India, 'Bonjour India' and the first edition of Festival of India in France, 'Namaste France'.

Welcoming June 21 as the 'International Day of Yoga' by the United Nations at Modi's behest, the two leaders welcomed the signing of Letter of Intent between the Central Council of Research in Ayurvedic Sciences, Ministry of Ayush and the University of Strasbourg for cooperation in Ayurvedic education and research through student, teacher and researcher-exchange programmes and technical publications.

France and India signed a MoU for cooperation in the field of skill development.

On health sector, the two sides decided to strengthen their partnership in the fields of non-communicable diseases, pharmaceutical industries and healthcare institutions; science and technology and sports.

Modi at UNESCO

In his address to UNESCO (United Nations Educational, Scientific and Cultural Organisation), Modi said that no organisation serves their case more than this one...UNESCO was among the first mission of the United Nations and India values the work of UNESCO very deeply. Whether it is sustainable development, climate change or peace and security, UNESCO always has a big role.

The Prime Minister, Shri Narendra Modi paying homage at the statue of Shri Aurobindo, at UNESCO, in Paris on April 10, 2015.

Modi enlisted some of the steps taken by him in line with objectives of UNESCO, which included imparting skills to the youth, education to every child in the remotest villages, women empowerment and making Digital India by launching digital literacy mission to connect each and every 600,000 villages.

Modi also elaborated on steps taken to preserve India's cultural heritage and spoke about a special scheme called PRASAD

(Pilgrimage Rejuvenation and Spirituality Augmentation Drive) launched in India for rejuvenation of pilgrim centres.

While observing that Culture must connect, not divide, our world, he said, "*We must turn deep into our culture, tradition, and religion; to overcome the rising tide of extremism, violence and divisions across the world. Therefore there was need to intensify exchanges between the youth of the world to sow the seeds of a more peaceful world.*"

"*Another issue attracting the attention of the world is global warming and climate change. India has set a target of adding 175,000 MW of clean and renewable energy in the next seven years*", he said and called for global public action to develop clean energy that is affordable and accessible to all.

During Modi's visit, as many as 20 agreements were signed ranging from nuclear energy, space, sports, economic relations, railways, energy, culture & heritage, tourism, education, Ayurveda and science & technology.

All the agreements are testimony to Modi's commitment to inclusive economic development and realise his vision of 'Make in India' besides addressing security concerns for establishing a peaceful environment.

Modi in GERMANY (April 12-14, 2015)

"We can only maintain a strong community if all member states have the will to carry out the necessary reforms."
—Angela Merkel

The political relations between India and Germany are harmonious. India was one of the first countries which had recognised the Federal Republic of West Germany and established a military mission in Berlin in 1948, which was converted into its embassy in 1952. British India had fought against Germany in the Second World War as a part of anti-Hitler coalition and lost more than 2000 soldiers according to some estimates.

The relations between the two countries also witnessed some setbacks at the time of 1971 Indo-Pakistan war, leading to creation of Bangladesh and also when India tested its first atomic bomb at Pokhran in 1974. However there has been a clear boost in the relations after the fall of the Berlin Wall and unification of Germany in 1990. The trade volume between the two countries also rose from €2.7 billion in 1990 to €13.4 billion by 2008.

The Prime Minister, Shri Narendra Modi unveiling the bust of Mahatma Gandhi, at Culemannstrasse, in Hannover, Germany on April 12, 2015. The Mayor of Hannover, Germany, Mr. Stefan Schostok is also seen.

The bilateral trade relations between India and Germany have remarkably increased over the years and both Indian and German firms have had their share of investment. In the post-recession, Indian exports to Germany have seen incredible growth in 2010, recording a total increase of 21.5 per cent. The figures of total exports have touched to €6.2 billion. India's exports to Germany in textile and IT sector are significant. India has been seeking from Germany easing of trade restrictions, particularly in the high-end technology sector to provide both the countries to work on and gain mutual benefit.

Exports from India to Germany mainly include leather products, agro-products, floricultural products, glass, chemical products, data processing, electronic and optical equipment, and machinery.

Modi's Visit to Germany

Prime Minister Modi began his engagements in Germany on April 12 by inaugurating the world's largest industrial fair at Hannover. As many as 350 companies from India and 120 CEOs were participating in the fair known as 'Hannover Messe', with India as Partner country.

Addressing the participants in the fair, Modi gave the firsthand account of his government's intent to accelerate economic growth, create jobs for youth, build world class industry and infrastructure, transform cities and villages; clean up the environment and improve the quality of life in India.

"*We will naturally pursue our goals on the strength of our own resources, skills and enterprise. But we know that we will be more successful when we do this in partnership with the world. For people of India, Germany is a valued partner, and, an enduring symbol of technology and innovation, quality and productivity,*" he said, thus inviting Germany for more investments and collaborations to help India achieve the goal. Modi specifically named Siemens, one of the German companies established long back in India for joint venture.

Describing his 'Make in India' initiative as a new national movement, the Prime Minister said. "*It covers the whole spectrum of our government, society and business...Our scale of transformation is vast, therefore, the opportunities we offer are huge.*"

The Prime Minister, Shri Narendra Modi at the Round Table Meeting with the German CEOs, in Hannover, Germany on April 12, 2015.

"*A stable economic environment along with strong fiscal discipline is being created to inspire confidence at home and abroad. Besides sweeping steps are being taken to reform policies and open up more to Foreign Direct Investments in key areas like insurance, construction, defence and railways. Railways sector is one where the country allows up to 100% foreign investment*", he said.

"*In addition, unnecessary regulations are being removed, and procedures simplified by eliminating multiple approvals and endless wait by using digital technology. Efforts are being made to build a tax regime, which is predictable, stable and competitive*", he informed.

Modi also elaborated on the country's plan on renewable and clean energy, setting a target of 75 Giga Watts, for the next seven years.

Inviting Germany to be a partner in making new India, Modi assured, "*India will do its part as an anchor of economic stability, an engine for growth and as a force of peace and stability in the world. So, let me invite you to do business and 'Make in India' – for India and the World.*"

Indo-German Business Summit

Inaugurating the Indo-German Business, Modi reiterated his 'Make in India' campaign and talked about India's redefined foreign policy, opening up foreign investments in various fields, including construction, renewable energy, railways, highways, modernising of existing ports, opening up regional ports to improve connectivity, financial services, like banks and insurance.

About 600 Indo-German Joint Ventures were presently operating in India and his presence at the Hannover Fair was primarily to inform Germans about more potential of economic collaboration between the two countries.

Allowing tax pass through for AIF (Alternative Investment Funds), rationalisation of capital gains of REITs (Real Estate Investment Trusts), modifications in PE (Permanent Establishment) norms and deferring the implementation of GAAR (General Anti Avoidance Rules) were some of the concessions made by India to improve the business environment further. He also spoke about proposed GST (Goods and Services Tax) Bill.

Such measures led to increase in FDI inflows by 36% between April 2014 and January 2015, as compared to same period the previous year. India has registered a growth rate of 7% which has been recognised by the international institutions like the World Bank, IMF (International Monetary Fund), UNCTAD (United Nations Conference on Trade and Development) and OECD (Organisation for Economic Co-operation and Development).

The Prime Minister, Shri Narendra Modi and the German Chancellor, Ms. Angela Merkel at the Joint Inauguration of the India Pavilion and the Joint Walk-About Make in India, in Hannover, Germany on April 13, 2015. The Minister of State for Commerce & Industry (Independent Charge), Smt. Nirmala Sitharaman is also seen.

Modi's Meeting with German Chancellor Angela Merkel

Modi had talks with Chancellor Merkel twice, one each in Hannover and Berlin in which the two leaders discussed ways to further strengthen the strategic relations between the two countries.

Besides, Modi informed that India was now the fastest growing economy, offering three fundamental facilities for investment – Demographic Dividend, Democracy and Demand – which no other country in the world possesses.

There are all possibilities to build a manufacturing hub in India. Germany's strength is manufacturing. India and Germany together can meet the world's demands in a better way, Modi told the Chancellor.

The Prime Minister, Shri Narendra Modi with the German Chancellor, Ms. Angela Merkel, during the Ceremonial Welcome, in Berlin, Germany on April 14, 2015.

The two sides also explored ways of expanding the dialogue on foreign policy and security issues and discussed the proposed visits of Germany's defence minister to India and India's external affairs minister to Germany before the Inter-Governmental Consultations scheduled in October 2015.

To provide further impetus to the strategic partnership between the two countries, it was decided to encourage their respective ministries and departments to take proactive steps to advance further collaborations in areas like manufacturing, skill development, urban development, environment, railways, cleaning of rivers, renewable energy, education, language and science & technology.

In the manufacturing sector, Germany agreed to utilise the momentum generated by India's participation in the Hannover Messe to foster stronger ties between business and industry on both sides in order to support India's 'Make in India' initiative.

The two leaders also decided to strengthen their efforts towards carrying on negotiations for an ambitious EU (European Union)-India Free Trade Agreement with a view to its early conclusion.

Addressing to the menace of terrorism gripping the world, the two leaders agreed that the United Nations must define terrorism and should pass a resolution in this regard in order to have a united global effort to contain it. In the meeting, Modi also sought Germany's support for India's claim for a permanent membership in the Security Council.

Modi in CANADA (April 14-17, 2015)

"We have in this country a federal government that increasingly is engaged in trying to determine which business, which regions, which industries will succeed, which will not through a whole range of economic development, regional development, corporate subsidization programs."
– **Stephen Harper**, Former Prime Minister of Canada

Indo-Canada Relations

The diplomatic relations between India and Canada date back to 1947. These are based on shared democratic values and strong people-to-people contacts. In recent years, both countries have worked to strengthen these relations made evident by several high-level visits – Dr. Manmohan Singh to Canada in 2010;

Prime Minister Stephen Harper to India in 2009 and 2012; and Governor General David Lloyd Johnston to India from February 22 to March 2, 2014.

In September 2013, the then External Affairs Minister, Salman Khurshid and Canadian Minister of Foreign Affairs, John Baird chaired the inaugural India-Canada Strategic Dialogue. Likewise, the first India-Canada Ministerial Energy Dialogue held in Ottawa the same year was co-chaired by the then Deputy Chairman of Planning Commission, Montek Singh Ahluwalia, and Joe Oliver, the then Canadian Minister of Natural Resources.

The Prime Minister, Shri Narendra Modi being warmly welcomed by the people of Indian Community, in Toronto, Canada on April 15, 2015.

The areas of Bilateral relations between the two countries are not limited to ministerial-level Strategic Dialogue and Energy Dialogue, but also encompass Security Dialogue,

Trade Policy Consultations, Economic and Financial Sector Policy Dialogue, Joint Working Group on Counter-terrorism, Science & Technology Committee, Environment Forum, Energy Forum, Steering Committee on Mining and Earth Sciences; and Joint Working Groups on ICTE (International Conference on Technology and Education), Education, Pulses, Plant Protection, Health, Agriculture and SPS issues. India and Canada have signed several agreements including the Air Services Agreement, Extradition Treaty, Mutual Legal Assistance Treaty and Agreement on Patents.

Taking the bilateral relations a step further, the two countries, in recent years, have also signed the agreements on Cooperation in Agriculture, Science & Technology, Environment, Nuclear, Social Security and Audio-Visual Co-Production.

These visits and agreements at their current levels fail to reflect the true potential of the commercial relationship between the two countries. During Prime Minister Harper's State visit to India in 2012, the two countries envisaged enhancement of bilateral trade between the two countries to US$15 billion by 2015. This aims at topping the bilateral trades of previous years that in 2012 was US$5.2 billion and was over US$5.7 billion in 2013, an increase of 7.69 per cent.

The cumulative Canadian FDI inflows into India have always remained less than the Indian FDI in Canada and the recent years have seen these investments increasing steadily, especially in the information technology, software and natural resources sectors. There was a slight dip in these investments in 2013. Currently in the pipeline is a Bilateral Investment Promotion Agreement that is being worked out between the two countries. The present focus of Canadian investors is in the fields of Indian banking, insurance, financial services sectors, engineering and consultancy services.

Both sides are engaged in negotiations for CEPA covering trade in goods, services, investment and trade facilitation. Separate MoUs exist to advance relations in the fields of energy, mining and agriculture. The branches and offices of State Bank of India, ICICI Bank, Government of India Tourist Office, Air India, OVL (ONGC Videsh Limited) and Jet Airways are operating in Canada. Jet Airways operate air services to Canada.

Leading Indian companies have presence in Canada such as Tata Steel, Aditya Birla Group, Reliance, Wipro, Infosys, TCS (Tata Consultancy Services), Mahindra Satyam, Essar Group, Jubilant, IFFCO (Indian Farmers Fertiliser Cooperative Limited) and GSFC (Gujarat State Fertilizers & Chemicals Ltd). Canada has established Trade Offices in Ahmedabad, Chennai, Hyderabad and Kolkata. Reputed Canadian companies such as Bombardier, SNC Lavalin, and CAE Inc. have a strong presence in India.

The Prime Minister, Shri Narendra Modi visiting the library of Canadian Parliament with the Prime Minister of Canada, Mr. Stephen Harper, in Ottawa, Canada on April 15, 2015.

Cultural Relations

Indian culture in the form of performing arts is very much in evidence in Canada, due to the large Indian diaspora settled in this country. A number of organisations promote Indian culture, especially the performing arts.

On the educational front, over 300 MoUs exist between Canadian and Indian higher education institutions for collaborative research and exchange programmes. This is because India is the second largest source of foreign students in Canada.

Indian Community

Over a million PIOs (Persons of Indian Origin) are permanently based in Canada with majority of them settled in Greater Toronto, Greater Vancouver, Montreal and Calgary. The bulk of these PIOs are from Punjab. That PIOs exercise political influence in the country is evident from the fact that there are eight Indo-Canadian MPs in the House of Commons and one in the Senate. Of these, two PIO MPs are Ministers of State in the Federal Government and one PIO MP is Parliamentary Secretary to the Foreign Minister.

Modi's Visit to Canada

Keeping in mind the robust bilateral relationship between the two countries, Modi spent three days in Canada visiting three states of Ottawa, Toronto and Vancouver from April 14 to 16. Modi was the first Indian Prime Minister visiting Canada after 42 years.

After his meeting with Canadian Prime Minister Stephen Harper, the two leaders issued a joint statement titled as 'New

Vigour, New Steps', indicating further push to their already good political as well as trade relations. The visit comprised extensive engagement with Canada's political, business, academic leaders and interactions with the Indian diaspora.

Modi elaborated on his 'Make in India' campaign and the two leaders focussed on expanding bilateral cooperation in key areas, including the economy, trade and investment, civil nuclear cooperation, energy, education and skills development, agriculture, defence and security, science & technology, innovation and space, culture, people-to-people ties, and regional and global issues.

Recognising the bilateral business and commercial linkages between the two countries, Modi put forward his inclusive economic agenda and the steps taken by his government to ease doing business in India. The initiatives like Affordable Housing for all by 2022 and 'Smart Cities' offered a significant collaborative opportunities for Indian and Canadian businesses and industry.

The two leaders acknowledged the importance of early finalisation of the Bilateral Foreign Investment Promotion and Protection Agreement to realise the shared objective of enhanced trade and investment cooperation between the two countries.

The Prime Minister, Shri Narendra Modi and the Prime Minister of Canada, Mr. Stephen Harper visiting the Laxmi Narayan Temple, in Vancouver, Canada on April 16, 2015.

A host of Canadian expertise in the fields of public-private partnerships, intelligent transportation systems, civil engineering and urban planning, water and wastewater management, pre-cast and wood construction, energy technology and efficiency and affordable housing were deemed indispensable for bilateral partnership for urban transformation and smart city development in India by the two leaders.

Two MoUs were signed between the two countries, one on the cooperation in rail transportation and the other for establishing a Joint Working Group to bring together key industry and government stakeholders to advance opportunities for cooperation in civil aviation.

For deepening India-Canada economic and financial relationship, the two sides agreed to establish a Finance Ministers Dialogue.

Civil Nuclear Cooperation

Both the leaders welcomed the signing of an agreement between the Department of Atomic Energy and Cameco of Canada for long-term supply of uranium to India to meet its energy needs, an area where the two countries have considerable potential. The importance of a collaborative programme in the field of Pressurised Heavy Water Reactor technology for mutual benefit and for the benefit of global nuclear energy needs was acknowledged by the two leaders. Canada appreciated India's initiative in setting up the India Nuclear Insurance Pool with potential participation of foreign companies.

Agreeing to take nuclear science and technology to the next level, the two Prime Ministers felt the need to establish mechanisms for long-term and mutually beneficial R&D

(Research and Development) collaboration in peaceful uses of nuclear energy.

Similarly the two leaders agreed to enhance cooperation in energy and resources, education and skills development, agriculture, science and technology, culture and people-to-people contact with more and more investments.

On Defence and Security Issue

India and Canada were unanimous that terrorism, extremism and radicalisation were posing security challenges to the peace, stability and prosperity. Condemning the menace in all of its manifestations, the two leaders pledged to obliterate terrorist safe havens and infrastructure, eradicate terrorist networks, their support systems and financing; and put a halt to the cross-border movement of terrorists.

Besides, the two leaders also recognised defence cooperation as an important element of the overall bilateral security cooperation.

People-to-People Ties

People-to-people ties between the two countries are the core element of robust ties between the two countries and Modi and Harper emphasised the need to further invigorate bilateral people-to-people contact. The leaders looked forward to the entry into force of the Canada-India Social Security Agreement on August 2015.

On Regional and Global Issues

The two leaders briefly talked on conflicts in Syria and Iraq and its implications for regional stability, situation in Afghanistan, cooperative efforts through G-20 to promote global growth and prosperity. Modi assured the Canadian leadership that he would look into their desire of having an observer status in the SAARC.

The two leaders also discussed the issue of non-proliferation and elimination of all weapons of mass destruction. Canada recognises India's non-proliferation record and continues to support India's early application and membership of the four multilateral export control regimes.

The Prime Minister, Shri Narendra Modi and the Prime Minister of Canada, Mr. Stephen Harper being presented Siropa (Robe of Honour) and Sword at the Gurudwara Khalsa Diwan, at Ross Street, Vancouver, in Canada on April 16, 2015.

Modi said at the joint press conference in Ottawa that he sought Canada's cooperation and investment in every area of India's national development priority – energy and infrastructure, manufacturing and skills, smart cities and agro-industry and research and education. Modi said, "*We are confident to conclude the Bilateral Investment Promotion and Protection Agreement very soon and also implement the road map to conclude the Comprehensive Economic Cooperation Agreement by September 2015.*"

"*The 13 agreements on skill development reflect my commitment to empower the youth of India with the world class skills for India and the global economy*", he said.

To support greater engagement of people to people contacts, India has also decided to liberalise policy for Canadians who will be issued Electronic Visa Authorisation for tourist visa. Besides they will also be eligible for ten-year visas now.

CHAPTER 4

MODI IN AUSTRALIA

Modi's Visit to AUSTRALIA (November 14 to 18, 2014)

"My guiding principle is that prosperity can be shared. We can create wealth together. The global economy is not a zero-sum game." —**Julia Gillard**, Former Prime Minister of Australia

Modi went to Australia for five days for paying a state visit and attending the G-20 Summit at Brisbane that was held from November 14 to 16. He is the first Indian Prime Minister who visited Australia after 28 years. He visited the cities of Brisbane, Sydney and Melbourne, addressed the joint session of the Australian Parliament and held bilateral meeting with his Australian counterpart Tony Abbott. He oversaw the signing of a number of Agreements and Memoranda of Understanding between the two countries. He also took the opportunity to meet various political leaders, academics, business people and sporting figures. He took time off to address the members of Australian Indian community. He visited research, cultural and historic institutions.

The two countries have a strong strategic and economic relationship. India has built upon several commonalities that it has with Australia, such as a strong, vibrant, secular and multicultural democracy. Other commonalities include English language, a free press, an independent judicial system, cricket and Indian students in Australian universities. This strong foundation based on commonalities has enabled the two countries for closer cooperation and interaction in various fields, akin to what India has developed with other Western countries.

With India's economic reforms in the 90s, the relationship between the two countries has grown in strength and importance, taking rapid strides in all areas – trade, energy and mining, science & technology, information technology, education and defence. Australia comes under India's extended neighbourhood. Addressing the Joint Session of Australian Parliament and his bilateral meeting with Australian Prime Minister Tony Abbott, Prime Minister Modi observed that the two countries were united by the ideals of democracy and lauded the progress made by Australia which was now one of the great nations of the world.

The Prime Minister, Shri Narendra Modi being greeted by the Prime Minister of Australia, Mr. Tony Abbott at the Opening Ceremony of the G-20 summit, in Brisbane, Australia on November 15, 2014.

Touching upon the 'Make in India' initiative, Modi said, "*India considers Australia as a 'vital' partner in its quest for progress and prosperity...India, a nation of more than a billion seeking development; Australia is a developed country of a few million people and vast resources.*" He further said, "*India is now the second fastest growing economy of the world and a nation of 800 million people below the age of 35 years. It is this energy and force of our youth that would lead to growth and transformation of India's economy to a higher trajectory.*"

Inviting Australia to be a major partner in India's inclusive development, Modi said, "*In every sector – agriculture, food processing, mining, infrastructure, manufacturing, finance, technology and energy – from providing funds and resources to technology and expertise; both working as partners and investors, Australia has immense opportunities to participate in India's progress.*"

Modi further added, "*In turn, India will be the answer to your search for new economic opportunities and your desire to diversify your global economic engagement, your sources for world class skills at home or for a manufacturing location abroad.*" He said, "*India's development, demography and demand provide a unique long term opportunity for Australia.*"

Modi informed about India's plans to develop 100 smart cities, revive heritage cities; build modern solid waste management and waste water treatment systems in 500 cities and cleaning up rivers. He said, "*This is part of our larger vision of a sustainable future for our country, and transforming the quality of life of our people in cities and villages, alike.*" Sounding confident of achieving the target with the vast talent and energy of 800 million youth, Modi said, "*India was looking forward to closer partnership with Australia in this mission.*"

Prime Minister Modi then shifted his focus on security, peace and stability in the region, observing that India and Australia can play their part in it by expanding their security cooperation and deepening their international partnerships in the region. He said, "*But, what we do need is to work together and with others to create environment and culture that promotes the currency of co-existence and cooperation; in which all nations, small and big, abide by international law and norms, even when they have bitter disputes.*"

The Prime Minister, Shri Narendra Modi paying tributes to Mahatma Gandhi after unveiling his statue, at Roma Street Parkland, in Brisbane, Australia on November 16, 2014.

Modi pointed out the need to support the process of economic integration across the region and an open global trading system that remains integrated, while cautioning to guard against regional trade initiatives becoming instruments of political competition. He further added that both India and Australia were members of several institutions that are critical for this region and the world. He said, "*We should coordinate more closely in East Asia Summit, G-20 and the Indian Ocean Region Association.*"

Speaking of terrorism, Modi informed about the changing character of terrorism which is expanding its reach. This is fuelled by the internet that enables the terrorists to recruit and call for violence. Its use also facilitates money laundering, drug trafficking and arms smuggling. In this regard, Modi wanted the two countries to deepen their bilateral security cooperation, in addition to a comprehensive global strategy for a global problem.

There was also need to ensure that outer space and cyber space remain instruments of connectivity and prosperity and not new frontiers of conflict. Modi called upon to address certain security challenges, like disasters in the region, proliferation, piracy, and the like and said that these are the areas where the two countries could work together on a full range.

In the meeting the two Prime Ministers also decided to establish a 'Framework for Security Cooperation' between India and Australia to reflect the deepening and expanding security and defence engagement between the two, and to intensify cooperation and consultation in areas of mutual interests. They reaffirmed that the strategic partnership between them was based on converging political, economic and strategic interests; a shared desire to promote regional and global peace, security and prosperity, and a commitment to democracy, freedom, human rights and the rule of law.

The Prime Minister described the Social Security Agreement as a 'positive development', saying it would make their business relations stronger, especially in the Services sector.

Modi informed his Australian counterpart about India's changing economic climate, saying, "*It will be a lot easier to convert opportunities into concrete outcomes.*" He added that there were huge opportunities for partnership in every area, such as agriculture, agro-processing, energy, finance, infrastructure, education and science & technology.

Acknowledging that reconstitution of the CEO Forum is an important step, he impressed upon the need for speeding up negotiations on the Comprehensive Economic Partnership Agreement. Modi urged for easier access for Indian business to the Australian market and quicker investment approvals.

It was mutually agreed that India would hold a 'Make in India' show in Australia in 2015 and Australia, a 'Business Week' in India.

The Prime Minister, Shri Narendra Modi concluded his speech with "Bharat Mata Ki Jai" at the Community Reception, at Allphones Arena, in Sydney, Australia on November 17, 2014.

Early finalisation of civil nuclear agreement that would enable Australia to participate in one of the most secure and safe nuclear energy programme in the world was also discussed by the two sides.

Recognising that exchanges in sports, tourism, education and culture were great source of strength for the relationship between India and Australia, the two countries decided to collaborate on a Sports University in India.

In addition to signing the framework for Security Cooperation, India and Australia also signed five more

Agreements for cooperation in various fields like social security, transfer of sentenced persons, combating narcotics, trafficking and developing police cooperation, arts and culture and tourism.

Bilateral Relations-Background

The two sides agreed to co-operate in various multilateral fora. Since both India and Australia are members of the G-20, Commonwealth, IORA (Indian Ocean Rim Association), ASEAN Regional Forum, Asia Pacific Partnership on Climate and Clean Development, and have participated in the East Asia Summits, Australia volunteered to extend its support to India's candidature in an expanded UN Security Council.

In 2008, Australia became an Observer in SAARC. The two countries are also members of FIP (Five Interested Parties) in the WTO (World Trade Organisation) context. Australia, being an important player in APEC, supports India's APEC membership.

Defence Cooperation

Defence cooperation between the two countries has expanded significantly in recent years. To this effect, a MoU on Defence Cooperation was signed as well as a Joint Declaration on Security Co-operation was issued. It was agreed that frequent visits by the Service Chiefs will be ensured, regular talks between the Naval, Air Force and Army counterparts of the two countries will take place, as well as, joint naval exercises will be held.

There is also a regular exchange at seminars in the two countries and at each other's training institutes. To this end, Australian Defence Minister Stephen Smith visited India in December 2011 for Defence Ministers' Dialogue and AK Antony, then India's Defence Minister, paid the first ever official visit by an Indian Defence Minister to Australia from June 4-5, 2013.

Commercial

A total of A$16.50 (US$17.68) billion was Australia's trade with India in goods and services in 2012-13. Whereas Indian exports to Australia amounted to A$3.38 (US$3.59) billion, Australia's exports to India totaled A$13.27 (US$14.09) billion. A decline of an annual average of nearly 11 per cent has been observed in Australia's exports to India over the past three years. As a result, India's ranking among Australia's export destinations has dropped from fourth to fifth during this period.

On the other hand, India has seen an annual average increase of nine per cent in exports of goods and services to Australia over the past three years. India's major imports from Australia are non-monetary gold, coal, copper, crude and fertilisers. India mainly exports gems and jewellery, machinery and textiles to Australia.

India constitutes the biggest export market for Australia for gold and chickpeas. Coal and copper ores take the second place in Australian export to India and lead and wool take the third.

Over 80 per cent of India's imports from Australia mainly comprise four products – coal, non-monetary gold, copper ores & concentrates and petroleum. In 2012-13, coal and gold were the major Indian imports from Australia.

Australia imported pearls and gems, jewellery, medicaments and passenger motor vehicles from India in 2012-13. These were India's major exports to Australia.

The India-Australia Joint Ministerial Commission was established in 1989 and has held 14 meetings to date. The last one was in New Delhi on 30 January 2013.

The major Indian IT companies that include Infosys, Satyam, Mahindra, TCS, HCL, Polaris Software Lab Ltd, Birlasoft, NIIT, ICICI Infotech, Wipro, Mahindra-British Telecom Ltd., among others, are showing a rapid growth and making their presence felt. The largest product development centre outside India of Satyam Mahindra is in Melbourne.

The Prime Minister, Shri Narendra Modi with the Prime Minister of Australia, Mr. Tony Abbott, Shri Sunil Gavaskar, Shri Kapil Dev and Shri V.V.S. Laxman at the Civic Reception hosted by the Australian PM, at MCG, Australia on November 18, 2014.

Tourism between the two countries is growing rapidly. With 1,73,000 tourists, India became the 11th largest contributor to tourism in 2013. This figure is expected to double by 2020. On the other hand, a total of 2,20,000 Australian tourists visited India in the same year. Air India also introduced direct flights between Delhi and Sydney/Melbourne from September 2013.

Indian Community

The Indian community in Australia, those who were born in India and are now settled there, is 2,95,000 strong, making India the third largest source of immigrants. The Indian community comprises teachers, doctors, accountants, engineers, researchers, etc. and contributes to Australia's economy in a big way. Australian universities are also popular amongst Indian students.

CHAPTER 5

MODI IN BRAZIL AND RUSSIA

Modi's Visit to BRAZIL (July 13-16, 2014)

"They have a joy for life in Brazil unlike any country I've ever seen." —**Morena Baccarin**

Prime Minister Narendra Modi attended the 6th BRICS Summit at Fortaleza in Brazil and also took the opportunity to meet Brazilian President Dilma Rousseff on one to one basis in the city, even though it was not Modi's State visit to Brazil. President Rousseff, on her part, ensured that Modi was accorded the State Honour at the Presidential Palace as a special gesture before their meeting over breakfast. Modi thanked her for the successful conclusion of the BRICS Summit and, in particular, for arranging meetings of BRICS leaders with South American leaders.

Modi termed Brazil the key global partner for India and emphasised the vast potential of India and Brazil as the two democracies and major emerging economies on bilateral cooperation and for strengthening each other in international forums to promote the interests of the developing world at large.

Modi highlighted the historical and cultural ties between the two countries by citing the examples of the Gir cows, Indian textiles and fruits that were brought to Brazil from India in the 18th and 19th centuries. The two leaders agreed on a number of initiatives that included expansion and diversification of trade and investment flows, boosting the cooperation in agriculture and dairy science, conventional and renewable energy, space research and application, defence, cyber security and environment conservation.

Promoting cooperation in international forums and multilateral institutions, including the G 20 was also agreed upon by the two leaders. As leaders of G 4 countries, Modi and President Rousseff expressed the urgency of reforms of the United Nations, including the Security Council, before the 70th anniversary of the UN in 2015.

Both the leaders oversaw the signing of the three agreements:

(i) MoU on cooperation in the field of environment;

(ii) MoU on cooperation in augmentation of Brazilian earth station for receiving and processing data from IRS (Indian Remote Sensing) Satellites;

(iii) MoU on cooperation in the establishment of a consultation mechanism on mobility and consular issues.

The Prime Minister, Shri Narendra Modi inaugurating the New Chancery Building of the Indian Embassy, at Brasilia, in Brazil on July 16, 2014.

The Prime Minister, Shri Narendra Modi inaugurated the New Chancery Building of the Indian Embassy, at Brasilia, in Brazil on July 16, 2014.

The bilateral and strategic nature of relationship between India and Brazil promotes collaborations in areas of agriculture, science & technology, defence, cultural and hydrocarbon. This has witnessed an increase in India-Brazil bilateral trade in the last two decades.

India's total bilateral trade with Brazil of US$10.6 billion in 2012 fell to US$9.5 billion dollars in 2013 decreasing by 10.7 per cent, although the trade in goods and services surged to an estimated US$12 billion.

Brazilian exports to India that had grown substantially from US$3.2 billion to US$5.6 billion in 2012 plummeted sharply in 2013 mainly due to the reduction in Brazilian crude oil exports.

Indian exports to Brazil that had seen a dip in 2012, recovered again past the US$6 billion mark owing mainly to the rise in the diesel exports in 2015. The dip was the result of continued robust domestic demand and decrease in Brazil's own production in 2013.

Brazil's share in Indian export market was about 2.6 per cent, whereas Brazil's share in Indian imports is about 1.3 per cent. Major portion of Indian exports to Brazil comprise manufactured products, commodities and semi-manufactured goods, whereas Brazil's exports to India are dominated by commodities, mainly crude oil.

Modi in RUSSIA (July 8-10, 2015)

"Our aims are absolutely clear: They are high living standard in the country and a secure, free and comfortable life."—**Vladimir Putin**, President of Russia

Relations with Russia are a key pillar of India's foreign policy and Russia has been a longstanding time-tested partner of India. Since the signing of "Declaration on the India-Russia Strategic Partnership" in October 2000 (during the visit of President Vladimir Putin to India), India-Russia ties have acquired a qualitatively new character with enhanced levels of cooperation in almost all areas of the bilateral relationship including political, security, trade and economy, defense, science and technology and culture. Under the Strategic Partnership, several institutionalized dialogue mechanisms operate at both political and official levels to ensure regular interaction and follow up on cooperation activities. During the visit of Russian President to India in December 2010, the Strategic Partnership was elevated to the level of a "Special and Privileged Strategic Partnership".

The Prime Minister, Shri Narendra Modi in bilateral meeting with the President of Russian Federation, Mr. Vladimir Putin, at Congress Hall, in Ufa, Russia on July 08, 2015.

Modi-Putin Meeting (*On the Sidelines of BRICS*)

Modi had a 40-minute meeting with the Russian President Vladimir Putin on the sidelines of the BRICS summit at the Russian city of Ufa. President Putin congratulated Modi on his victory in the recent elections. Modi, who had met Putin in 2001 in Moscow, said that India's relationship with Russia was time tested and had grown since India's independence.

The discussion in the meeting ranged from strengthening strategic partnership in nuclear, defence and energy sectors to further enhancing people-to-people contacts between the two countries. Putin assured Modi that Russia places its relations with India high in the strategic framework and said he considered nuclear power project as a symbol of India-Russia relations. Modi expressed his desire for a liberal visa regime, especially for students travelling to Russia for studies.

Modi invited President Putin to visit a nuclear construction site outside Delhi, an apparent reference to the Kudankulam II project, when he comes to attend the annual summit dialogue in December. Putin's response to this invitation was, *"It's a good idea"*.

The Prime Minister, Shri Narendra Modi being traditionally welcomed on his arrival at Russian city of Ufa, on July 08, 2015.

Speaking in Hindi, Modi remarked, "*Even a child in India if asked to name India's best friend will name Russia, because Russia has always been with India in times of crisis.*"

Modi fondly remembered that he visited Russia's Astrakan region, so much like India, during his early days as Chief Minister of Gujarat. Astrakan region has ties with Gujarat.

Appreciating Putin's speech at the BRICS summit, Modi said that he was clear on issues pertaining to reforms in the UN Security Council and international financial organisations.

CHAPTER 6

INDIAN OCEAN OUTREACH & PACIFIC ISLANDS

Seychelles, Mauritius and Fiji

The IOR (Indian Ocean Region), which is long being considered as India's nautical backyard, is steadily turning into a hotspot, thanks to growing Chinese strategic presence over the region's numerous strategically located archipelagos. To counter the recent moves made by China for realising President Xi's pet Maritime Silk Road project, India started to reach out to its maritime neighbours in the IOR with proposals of enhanced economic and security cooperation.

The policy towards IOR started to unfold during Sri Lankan President's visit to New Delhi in early February 2015. Following this, Modi embarked on a three-nation *yatra* (pilgrimage) to Mauritius, Seychelles and Sri Lanka. Though Maldives was also initially part of this outreach, but recent political turmoil in that country led to last-minute cancellation of the scheduled visit.

Modi has a very strong conviction that unless there is peace in the Indian Ocean and countries lying in its vicinity, his dream of establishing peace and prosperity in the region would remain unfulfilled. He also knows the potential of ocean energy and the importance of trade through the seas for faster development of all countries. Keeping this in view he embarked upon a five-day tour (March 10-14, 2015) of the three Indian Ocean Island countries – Seychelles, Mauritius and Sri Lanka – that hold importance for India for both security and economic reasons. This also reflected the newly defined India's foreign policy priorities for immediate and extended neighbourhood. The visit to Sri Lanka has already been covered in the previous chapter.

Modi's Visit to SEYCHELLES (March 10-11, 2015)

"India-Seychelles relations have been characterized by close friendship, understanding and cooperation."
—**Pratibha Patil**, Former President of India

Seychelles was the first country in the Indian Ocean where Modi went on a two-day visit starting March 10, 2015. India has a strong security partnership with this country, based on mutual trust and confidence. The visit holds significance for more reasons than one, it being the first visit by an Indian Prime Minister since 1981. During his stay, Modi held talks with Seychelles President Michel, mainly on maritime security in the region and assured all assistance to him for development of his country's security capabilities.

The Prime Minister, Shri Narendra Modi unveiling the plaque and operationalisation of Radar for the CSRS India-Seychelles Cooperation Project, in Mahe, Seychelles on March 11, 2015.

The Prime Minister, Shri Narendra Modi with the President of Seychelles, Mr. James Michel, at State House, in Mahe, Seychelles on March 11, 2015.

Modi launched the Coastal Surveillance Radar Project by announcing that India would give one Dornier aircraft to Seychelles for advance security surveillance in the region.

Modi outlined three steps for the security of the island and of the vast expanse of water around it. Touching upon the agreement between the two countries on hydrographic survey, he said that it would add a new dimension to their maritime cooperation. He expressed his wish to see at the earliest Seychelles becoming a full partner in the maritime security cooperation between India, Maldives and Sri Lanka.

Underlying the importance of comprehensive cooperation in the Indian Ocean Region, the two countries agreed to support a more active and productive IORA.

The two countries signed another agreement on the development of infrastructure on the Assumption Island. This, Modi hoped, would further boost the partnership between the two countries.

Appreciating Seychelles for being a leader in advancing the concept of Blue Economy, Modi said Ocean economy was indispensable to meeting future challenges. The two sides agreed to establish a Joint Working Group to expand cooperation in this field. This will also help to learn more about maritime ecology and resources.

The two sides stressed the need to expand trade and investment relations and Modi suggested information technology as one such field. Modi outlined some of the steps taken by his government to facilitate investment and speedup the development. India extended grant of three-month free visas and the facility of visa on arrival to Seychelles citizens. Seychelles supports India at all international forum and India's claim for a permanent membership in the UN Security Council.

Modi's Visit to MAURITIUS (March 11-13, 2015)

"Mauritius was made first, and then heaven and that heaven was copied after Mauritius." —**Mark Twain**

Mauritius and India have a deep bond in terms of heritage, cultural and economic ties. This is mainly due to the reason that this country has a sizeable population of Indian origin.

Modi arrived in Mauritius on a two-day state visit on March 12, the day he was scheduled to be the Chief Guest of the country's National Day. The same day, he was invited to address Mauritius National Assembly. He also commissioned an OPV (Offshore Patrol Vessel) 'Barracuda' for the National Coast Guard of Mauritius.

Thanking Mauritius to invite him as Chief Guest on its National Day that according to him was an honour for the 1.25 billion people of India, Modi said 'Barracuda' that sailed from Kolkata across the great arc of the Indian Ocean, brought with her goodwill and greetings of the people of India. He said that she will help to make the Indian Ocean safer and more secure. This will also help Mauritius in fulfilling its international responsibility.

The Prime Minister, Shri Narendra Modi attends the National Day celebrations in Mauritius on March 12, 2015. The Prime Minister of Mauritius, Sir Anerood Jugnauth is also seen.

Ocean Security

Modi informed that Indian Ocean is critical to the future of the world, as it bears two-thirds of the world's oil shipments, one-third of its bulk cargo; and half of its container traffic. Over three-fourths of its traffic goes to other regions of the world. The vast Indian Ocean Region hosts over 40 states and nearly 40 per cent of the world population. It touches Australia, South East Asia, South Asia, West Asia and the eastern seaboard of Africa. Therefore, the Indian Ocean has come at the centre of global attention more than ever before.

Modi said, "*We all prosper when the seas are safe, secure and free for all. It is therefore our collective responsibility to ensure that our seas are safe, secure and free.*"

The Prime Minister, Shri Narendra Modi offering floral tribute at the Gandhi Statue at Mahatma Gandhi Institute of Mauritius, in Mauritius on March 12, 2015.

India, Indian Ocean and Mauritius

Apprising that Indian Ocean Region is amongst India's top policy priorities, Modi informed that India has about 90 per cent of its trade volume and 90 per cent of its oil imports through sea and has a coastline of 7500 km, 1200 islands and 2.4 million square km of Exclusive Economic Zone. He said that India's vision for Indian Ocean Region is rooted in advancing cooperation in the region; and using collective capabilities for the benefit of all in our common maritime home.

Modi emphasised the need for India and Mauritius to join hands to ensure a safe, secure and stable Indian Ocean Region and to further deepen economic and security cooperation with maritime neighbours and island states. While describing strong maritime relationship between India and Mauritius, he said, "*Collective action and cooperation will advance peace and security in the maritime region and make them better respond to emergencies*".

Terrorism and Piracy

Expressing concern over the increasing incidents of terrorism and sea piracy, Modi said, "*Terror has visited us from sea. Piracy has taken its toll on lives and trade on a scale that seemed beyond belief in the modern era. It was necessitated to increase efforts to strengthen regional mechanisms for maritime cooperation to deal with piracy terrorism and other crimes; to maintain marine safety and natural disasters. India had already begun maritime security cooperation with Maldives, Sri Lanka and hoped Mauritius and Seychelles and other nations in the region would also join them.*"

Sustainable Development

Modi stressed that all countries should jointly promote greater collaboration in trade, tourism and investment; infrastructure development, marine science and technology, sustainable fisheries, protection of marine environment and overall development of ocean and blue economy. According to him, this would lead to creation of more jobs and more prosperity.

Climate Change and Indian Ocean Rim Association (IORA)

While expressing concern over illegal fishing and oil spills that affect economies, Modi said that climate change was not an issue of debate, but a serious threat to the existence of those who lived by the ocean. He called for a more concerted and fair global action to address this challenge.

On its part, the Indian Ocean Rim Association can become an important instrument for pursuing the vision of a sustainable and prosperous future in the region. Modi suggested forming a strong grouping around the Indian Ocean on the line of grouping of states around the land masses.

Modi's Address to the National Assembly of Mauritius

Addressing the National Assembly, Modi praised Mauritius for maintaining a great harmony among diverse population of over a million people and its efforts to diversify economy. He described Mauritius "*as a leader in the Indian Ocean Community and as a bridge to Africa.*"

The Prime Minister, Shri Narendra Modi at the Joint Commissioning of Offshore Patrol Vessel (OPV) Barracuda, at the Port Louis Harbour, in Mauritius on March 12, 2015.

Inclusive Economic Agenda

Modi asked both India and Mauritius, who had a stable platform, to speed up economic development. He elaborated on his clear vision of inclusive development that aims to:

(i) increase economic growth; reform economy and transform the lives of people; and

(ii) create opportunities for the most excluded youth, the remotest farmer and the farthest village.

Assuring all assistance to Mauritius for development, Modi felt privileged to be a development partner of Mauritius. "*We will always be ready to do more,*" he said, while promising to look into the issue of abuse of double taxation. He had already announced a new Line of Credit of US$500 million for the development of civilian projects in Mauritius.

The Prime Minister, Shri Narendra Modi at Ganga Talao, in Mauritius on March 12, 2015.

Former Prime Minister Atal Bihari Vajpayee had supported the construction of first cyber city in Mauritius in 2003, as a symbol of thriving economic partnership between the two countries. Modi said India would support another cyber city in Mauritius. He also referred to India's collaboration in meeting the country's petroleum requirements. He promised to begin the construction of petroleum storage facility in Mauritius in order to strengthen its position as a regional economic hub.

Marine Economy

Appreciating Mauritius for its development of ocean economy that ranged from fishing to tourism, Modi said India was also highly dependent on the seas and continues to make efforts to develop its marine economy. He said that oceans hold vast potential to boost prosperity and meet the challenges of the world. At the same time, he expressed India's confidence in preserving the delicate ecosystem of the oceans and said that he values the oceans that have an imprint in the shape of 'blue chakra' in its national flag.

Climate Change

Modi appreciated Mauritius for being a leading international voice on climate change, not just an advocate for island states, but also for the sake of collective future. He assured that India would like to associate with Mauritius *"for a more resolute global action"* against climate change. Modi informed that to this end, India has set an ambitious target of 100 Gigawatts of solar energy and 60 Gigawatts of wind energy by 2022. This is not only to increase its energy efficiency, but also to provide the cleanest form of energy.

Indo-Mauritius Relationship

Noting that security partnership was a great pillar of the relationship between India and Mauritius, Modi emphasised the need for a comprehensive partnership between them on security, economic, cultural, scientific and people-to-people ties in the region and sought the country's support for reform of the United Nations.

As many as five agreements/MoUs were signed between India and Mauritius on March 11, 2015, during the Prime Minister's visit. These included MoU on Ocean Economy which provides an extensive framework for cooperation in the field of Ocean economy, a novel and critical area of sustainable development in the Indian Ocean Region; MoU on Cultural Cooperation that is a three-year programme (2015-2018) and envisages exchange of cultural troupes, training in fine arts, preservation of cultural heritage, promotion of Indian languages and exchange of students; MoU on improving Sea and Air Transportation that envisages setting up and upgradation of infrastructure for improving sea and air connectivity; and MoU on cooperation in the field of Traditional System of medicine and Homeopathy.

A protocol was also signed by the Agriculture Ministries of both the countries to facilitate import of fresh mango fruit from India.

Modi's State Visit to FIJI (November 19, 2014)

"Our Fiji today is a new Fiji where individual freedom is protected and not a Fiji solely for Fijians." – **Frank Bainimarama**, Prime Minister of the Republic of Fiji

Modi timed his Fiji visit as soon as democracy was restored in the island country after a period of 8 long years. He became the first Indian head of government to visit Fiji after Indira Gandhi visited it in 1981, more than 33 years ago for attending the 'Forum for India-Pacific Island Cooperation', along with the leaders of all 14 PIC (Pacific Island Countries) that comprise Cook Islands, Kingdom of Tonga, Tuvalu, Republic of Nauru, Republic of Kiribati, Vanuatu, Solomon Islands, Samoa, Niue, Republic of Palau, Federated States of Micronesia, Republic of Marshall Islands, Fiji and Papua New Guinea.

Modi's initiative is seen to be a major diplomatic outreach to the pacific community who continue to support India's candidature for a permanent seat in a reformed UN Security Council.

In addition to the scheduled bilateral meeting, Modi put on his agenda meeting with heads of state/government from 14 Pacific Island States in Suva with a view to enhance India's engagement in the region. Modi proposed FIPIC (Forum for India-Pacific Islands Cooperation) be held on a regular basis. Expressing India's keenness to work closely with PIC for their development, Modi spelled out a number of measures to strengthen India's partnership in the region.

These measures included setting up of a 'Special Adaptation Fund' of US$1 million for adapting climate change vis-a-vis clean energy; establishing a 'trade office' in India; 'Pan Pacific Islands e-network' to improve digital connectivity; introducing visa on arrival facility at Indian airports for all the 14 Pacific Island countries; 'space cooperation' in space technology applications; and imparting 'training to diplomats' from Pacific Island countries to increase mutual understanding. Modi offered to host the leaders attending next summit in 2015 in any of India's coastal towns.

The Prime Minister, Shri Narendra Modi at the interaction with civil society groups, at Fiji National University, in Suva, Fiji on November 19, 2014.

The Prime Minister, Shri Narendra Modi in a group photo with the Pacific Island Leaders at the Forum for India-Pacific Island Cooperation, in Suva, Fiji on November 19, 2014.

From the very beginning, India had a special affinity towards Fiji, as it has a large chunk of Indian origin population. India remained committed to the development and resurgence of the archipelago nation by extending US$50.4 million Line of Credit in July 2002 for modernising the country's sugar factories. Besides the sugar industry, the two countries have identified a few other key areas for bilateral collaboration, these being IT, tourism and solar energy. Tourism forms the pillar of Fiji's economy, as the country attracts a lot of tourists from across the globe.

In keeping with the success achieved in the pan-Africa Project, Modi proposed to develop Pan Pacific Islands Project for telemedicine and tele-education. He informed that India was already working on a solar energy project with the Pacific Islands at the community level and proposed to develop regional hubs.

Augmenting people-to-people contact with all countries is one of Modi's priority areas. He took this opportunity to announce an increase in Grant-in-Aid for community projects to each

Pacific Island Country from the current US$125,000 annually to US$200,000 annually.

The Prime Minister, Shri Narendra Modi being given traditional welcome, in Suva, Fiji on November 19, 2014.

Accepting the longstanding request to promote trade between India and the Pacific Island Countries, Modi expressed his readiness to support the setting up of a Trade Office at an existing diplomatic representation in New Delhi. These countries would also be provided complimentary space during exhibitions, organised by the India Trade Promotion Organisation, to showcase their products.

Modi, however, emphasised the need to find complementariness in their trade and said India could be an important source of low cost medicines. He said, "*We can do joint research in traditional medicine, explore options of developing healthcare facilities for the benefit of people in the region.*"

Modi took the initiative to offer Indian technical experts in the fields of agriculture, healthcare and IT to these countries and invited diplomats from these countries for training in India. In this context, he said the Foreign Service Training Institutes would organise training programmes for the diplomats from these countries.

The Prime Minister, Shri Narendra Modi being welcomed by the Prime Minister of Fiji, Mr. Frank Bainimarama at traditional welcome ceremony, in Suva, Fiji on November 19, 2014.

In concluding his speech, Modi offered cooperation in use of Space technology applications for improving the quality of life of the people and communications. He said, "*We can look at the possibilities of sharing data that could be used for monitoring climate change, disaster risk reduction and management, resource management.*"

Modi oversaw the signing of three MoUs with the Fijian government. These were:

(i) On cooperation on exchange of information on structure and content of training programmes for diplomats;

(ii) On earmarking of land for the Diplomatic Missions in respective capitals;

(iii) For extending a Line of Credit for establishing a Co-Generation Plant in Fiji.

CHAPTER 7

INDIA AND MULTILATERAL FORUMS

BRICS, ASEAN, G-20 and SAARC

Prime Minister Narendra Modi had been in Brazil to attend the 6th BRICS Summit at Fortaleza on July 15, 2014, had gone to Myanmar to attend 12th India-ASEAN Summit at Nay Pyi Taw from November 11 to 13, 2014, attended the G-20 Summit at Brisbane in Australia from November 14 to 18, 2014 and the 18th SAARC Summit at Kathmandu in Nepal from November 25 to 27, 2014.

At all the regional and international fora, Prime Minister conveyed to the delegates that India is a fast-growing economy which offers great opportunities for investments in many sectors, including infrastructure, IT, health, defence, energy, transport, road construction, agriculture, water, education and tourism.

Besides he emphasised on the need for peace and tranquillity in the world, maritime security, collective efforts to fight terrorism and reforms in the UN Security Council to make it more representative.

Modi at BRICS

Speaking on 'Sustainable Development & Inclusive Growth' at the 6th BRICS Summit at Fortaleza, Brazil, Modi cautioned about the uncertainty and challenging environment of global economy, saying recovery was still fragile despite improved prospects.

Speaking of political conflict and persisting weakness in major economies, Modi expressed his concern over it and cautioned all to prepare for a new bout of financial turmoil. He said that growth may get affected by the current developments in Iraq and West Asia region. He said, "*An open, rule-based, international trading regime was also critical for economic growth, particularly for developing world.*"

Drawing parallel between the theme of the Summit and that of his government, Prime Minister said, "*Inclusive growth is a challenge for a country like India with its vast social, regional and economic diversity.*"

The Prime Minister, Shri Narendra Modi with the President of Brazil, Ms. Dilma Rousseff, the President of the People's Republic of China, Mr. Xi Jinping, the President of the Russian Federation, Mr. Vladimir Putin and the President of the Republic of South Africa, Mr. Jacob Zuma, during BRICS official photo, at the Sixth BRICS Summit, at Ceara Events Centre, in Fortaleza, Brazil on July 15, 2014.

Modi told the delegates that to make his agenda of inclusive growth a success, his government was aiming to empower people with skills and opportunities for jobs, and also focussing on investing heavily in infrastructure, affordable housing, healthcare, education and clean energy.

Modi said, "*BRICS wields enough horizontal influence to compel the world to take its notice, but it lies in the deepening of our bonds.*" He called upon the member countries to focus on 'further decentralising' this powerful forum. He added, "*We must go beyond the Summit and Leader-centric deliberations; champion sub-national level exchanges. We must encourage engagement between our states, cities and other local bodies.*"

Modi stressed upon the fact that BRICS should promote people-to-people contact, exchange of youth delegations, encourage our languages and consider establishing massive open online courses for making quality education accessible to all. "*We can explore the idea of establishing a BRICS University*", he said.

Certain other possible initiatives among BRICS countries can include health, education, agriculture, resource management, urban development, cooperation between small and medium enterprises and tourism.

Modi, while addressing the Summit on 'Political Coordination: International Governance and Regional Crises', stressed the need for restoring a climate of peace and stability for global progress and prosperity. Referring to the turbulence and conflict from Afghanistan to Africa, he said that it was causing serious instability "*that is fast seeping across borders.*"

Modi said, "*The World must unite to support Afghanistan in its fight against terrorism and in building a peaceful, stable, democratic and prosperous country.*"

Modi added that the situation in West Asia is similar and poses a grave threat to regional and global peace and security, especially what is happening in Syria continues to cause serious concern. He assured all that India was prepared to take part in any peace process.

On Israel-Palestine issue, Modi said, "*India would support a negotiated solution.*"

He appealed for collective pressure on States by cooperation among BRICS countries to thwart terrorism by denying sanctuaries and support to terrorists. He emphasised the need for an early adoption by the United Nations of the draft Comprehensive Convention on International Terrorism. Similarly BRICS countries shall lead in preserving cyber spaces, as a global common good.

Modi at ASEAN SUMMIT

At Nay Pyi Taw in Myanmar, Prime Minister was more business-like in his approach. He was of the view that ASEAN countries and India could jointly work on many projects including solar energy, since several ASEAN countries had high radiation levels in terms of solar energy. This can help promote cooperation, research and collaboration in the field of solar energy that is clean energy.

Modi expressed his desire that the domain of RCEP (Regional Comprehensive Economic Partnership) be widened to also include services and not merely be restricted to trade in goods.

Giving the example of Singapore and Korea, Modi praised Singapore's thrust towards urban rejuvenation and Korea's proven industrial competence. He felt that these could be included by India in its programmes.

The Prime Minister, Shri Narendra Modi in a group photo with the Heads of State/Government of 12th ASEAN-India Summit, in Nay Pyi Taw, Myanmar on November 12, 2014.

Prime Minister also referred to India-Malaysia cooperation in the field of security, intelligence sharing as a model which can be built on by other countries, while touching on issues relating to terrorism, drug trafficking and gun running.

Modi at EAS (EAST ASIA SUMMIT)

November 2014 saw Modi proceeding to Nay Pyi Taw, Myanmar to participate in the 9th East Asia Summit, which was his second major multilateral event after BRICS held in July. Describing the importance of the EAS in managing regional security, Modi mentioned, "*No other forum brings together such a large collective weight of global population, youth, economy and military strength. Nor is any other forum so critical for peace, stability and prosperity in Asia-Pacific and the world.*"

A total of 18 countries comprise EAS, an ASEAN led dialogue forum. Of these countries, 10 are core ASEAN nations, along with Japan, China, South Korea, India, Australia, New Zealand, Russia and United States. EAS has assumed importance over the years as a multilateral body in the Asia pacific region for discussing security, trade and commerce, environment and others. EAS is different from APEC, which is purely economic in nature.

Modi also made reference towards South China Sea and asked the global community for respecting maritime norms and regulations and stressed on the importance of maintaining free and secured sea-lines of communication for regular trade and commerce.

Modi said, "*In a world of interdependence and globalisation, there is no option but to follow international laws and norms. This also applies to maritime security. For this reason, following international law and norms is important for peace and stability in South China Sea as well*".

Modi also urged the EAS member countries to tackle the menace of terrorism in the region. He also suggested the role all EAS member states could play to showcase the joint effort of the block by re-opening Nalanda University.

A detailed discussion also took place on the issue of Regional Comprehensive Economic Partnership (RCEP) during the summit in addition to other issues.

Modi took the opportunity to hold several bilateral meetings with Russian Premier Dmitry Medvedev, Philippines President Benigno Aquino III, Chinese Premier Li Keqiang and Indonesian President Joko Widodo.

Modi at G-20

At Brisbane, in Australia, India had an ambitious multi-pronged agenda for the G-20 Summit that ranged from deploying global surpluses for infrastructure development and inclusive development to energy efficiency and global action to mitigate Ebola. Topping the list was lifting of the global economic growth by 2% – the overarching goal of the Brisbane Summit – and blending the growth with sustainable development and job creation.

Modi divulged India's core goals at the Summit as global economic growth and stability, stable financial markets, global trading regimes and employment generation.

He underlined India's development priorities and enlisted the global support for accelerating *"the creation of next generation infrastructure, which includes digital infrastructure, ensuring access to clean and affordable energy."*

Promoting inclusive development agenda and enhanced infrastructure investment, Modi referred to his 'Make in India' initiative and asked the world to contribute towards making India a manufacturing powerhouse and an economic dynamo.

Besides raising other issues which Prime Minister had mentioned in other multilateral forums, Modi pitched strongly for bringing back black money and said, "*...it is very important. India is doing its level best to get it and has been able to get a very significant part of that.*" He highlighted the importance of international cooperation against black money.

The Prime Minister, Shri Narendra Modi meeting the President of the European Council, Mr. Herman Van Rompuy, in Brisbane, Australia on November 14, 2014.

Prime Minister also spoke for inclusion of transparency clause, talking about base erosion and profit sharing action plan to modernise international tax rules. His views were reflected in the final communiqué which read, "*We are committed to finalising this work in 2015, (that is the base erosion and profit shifting) including transparency of tax-payer's specific rulings found to constitute harmful tax practices.*"

On the issue of climate change, Modi acknowledged that India is faced with huge challenges in dealing with climate change "*which is a reality as a result of past emission.*"

Pressing for adaptation clause to be included in the United Nations Framework Convention on Climate Change, Modi said "*if the past emission is a reality, the adaptation is a necessity, therefore we are insisting on that and we could get that on board.*"

A strong case was made out at the Summit about the need to reduce cost of remittances, keeping in view the welfare of the 25 million Indian diaspora spread across continents, who sent the largest amount of money back home – US$70 billion.

"*No other country sends that much. That was attracting bank charges as high as 10% in many countries. We have now agreed to bring it down below 5%. We were still insisting that it should be with the timeline of 2016, but at least we are focussing on that. This is taken as a priority*", Union Minister Suresh Prabhu told the media. This also goes to the initiative of Modi that even one per cent reduction in costs of remittances would mean additional US$700 million for India at the current remittances.

Appreciating the inclusion of a provision on food security in the trade facilitation agreement of the Bali Action Plan, Modi conveyed his commitment to implement the Bali Package, as also quickly define this WTO work programme on the remaining issues of the Doha Development Agenda at the earliest to get the negotiations going once again.

Modi said, "*Doha Round was touted as the Development Round, but it looks like for a while we were focusing only on trade facilitation. So, India has taken a very firm, but very principled stand and I am glad that it is now vindicated by all the countries, including G-20 which says that food security will be one of the important parts.*"

On energy issue, the delegates at G-20 welcomed Modi's call for creating a global centre for dealing with renewable energy to find solutions.

The next subject that Modi touched was on reforms and he explained what reforms really meant. He said reforms should be people-centric, benefiting people and not benefitting the corporate and the governments alone. Besides these should not be leader driven, but institutionalised. This statement was highly appreciated at the Summit.

Modi at SAARC

Prime Minister Modi, who had stumped the world with his masterstroke of inviting the SAARC leaders at his swearing-in ceremony in New Delhi in May 2014, again took the opportunity to hold bilateral meetings with the Prime Ministers of Bhutan and Bangladesh, and the Presidents of Afghanistan, Maldives and Sri Lanka on the sidelines of the SAARC Summit in Kathmandu.

According to the official spokesperson, these leaders congratulated Modi *"for his forward looking vision of South Asian Cooperation."*

In his address to the 18th SAARC Summit, Prime Minister said, *"Nowhere in the world are collective efforts more urgent than in South Asia; and, nowhere else is it so modest. Big and small, we face the same challenges – a long climb to the summit of development."*

He felt that barriers of boundaries inhibit progress; international partnerships add speed to it. *"Because, in life of an individual or a nation, a good neighbourhood is a universal aspiration,"* he said.

Although SAARC in the past 30 years achieved a lot, yet *"we hear two reactions – cynicism and scepticism. Today, less than five per cent of the region's global trade takes place between us. Even at this modest level, less than 10 per cent of the region's internal trade takes place under SAARC Free Trade Area"*, he remarked.

Modi further pointed out that Indian companies were investing billions abroad, *"but less than 1% into our region. Talking about poor connectivity between SAARC countries"*, Modi said, *"It is harder to travel within our region than to Bangkok or Singapore.... How much have we done in SAARC to turn our natural wealth into shared prosperity, or our borders into bridgeheads to a shared future."*

The Prime Minister, Shri Narendra Modi addressing the inaugural session of the 18th SAARC Summit, in Kathmandu, Nepal, on November 26, 2014.

He referred to several initiatives and collaborations that had taken place in the area of people-to-people contact between India and the neighbouring countries of Bangladesh, Nepal, Bhutan and Sri Lanka, and also with Pakistan. "*India*", he said, "*had given duty free access of up to 99.7 per cent to the goods of five South Asian partners and had the privilege to provide assistance of nearly US$8 billion in South Asia over a decade.*"

"As SAARC, *we however failed to move with the speed that our people expected*", Modi said, emphasising the need to "*shrink the distance between our producers and consumers and use the most direct routes of trade.*"

Modi listed out the other areas where SAARC countries could jointly work. These were infrastructure development, energy, road, rail and air connectivity, health and information technology.

On security and terrorism issue, he highlighted, "*SAARC needed the strong foundation of a secure South Asia. If SAARC countries were sensitive to each other's security, and the lives of their people, they would have to deepen friendships, spur cooperation and advance stability in our region.*"

Modi informed all about gifting a satellite for the SAARC region that would promote education, telemedicine, disaster response, resource management, weather forecasting and communication. He was positive that this would benefit the people of these countries.

The Prime Minister, Shri Narendra Modi addressing the Plenary Session of the Sixth BRICS Summit, at Ceara Events Centre, in Fortaleza, Brazil on July 15, 2014.

Modi concluded his speech with the statement, "*For India, our vision for the region rests on five pillars – trade, investment, assistance, cooperation in every area, contacts between our people – and, all through seamless connectivity. This is the call of our times. This is the age of social media, where boundaries matter little. There is a new awakening in South Asia; a new recognition of interlinked destinies and a new belief of shared opportunities.*"

CHAPTER 8

INDIA & COMMONWEALTH OF INDEPENDENT STATES (CIS) COUNTRIES

Prime Minister Narendra Modi's visit to five Central Asian countries demonstrated the importance India attaches to the region. As Modi had said, "*We see an important place for Central Asia in India's future. We can reinforce each other's economic progress. Sustainable development is important for both. We can contribute to cooperation and integration across the different regions of Asia.*"

Modi in UZBEKISTAN (July 7, 2015)

"*When you look at the totality of what Uzbekistan has been doing, they've been a very valuable partner and ally in the global war on terror.*" —**Bryan Whitman**, US Principal Deputy Assistant Secretary of Defense for Public Affairs

India-Uzbekistan Relations

It may come as a surprise to many that India from antiquity had cultural and religious ties with Uzbekistan. This country was the gateway for Buddhism to spread into China and further on to Central Asia. Babur, the first Mughal king who founded the Mughal dynasty in India, was said to be an Uzbek. Indian merchants based in Samarkand and Bukhara influenced the local economy of Uzbekistan. India's close cultural links with Uzbekistan had a deep influence on the Indian architecture, dance, music and cuisine. These ties continue till date and Indian movies remain popular in the country.

The Prime Minister, Shri Narendra Modi shaking hands with the Prime Minister of Uzbekistan, Mr. Shavkat Miromonovich Mirziyoyev after they paid tributes at the National Monument of Independence and Humanism in Tashkent, Uzbekistan on July 07, 2015.

The agreement on Trade and Economic Cooperation signed in May 1993 between India and Uzbekistan continues to govern the trade relations between the two countries. The Agreement has under its ambit various initiatives, such as mutual MFN

(Most Favoured Nation) treatment; promotion of economic, industrial, scientific and technical cooperation, including in the field of training of personnel; active participation of small and medium sized enterprises in bilateral economic cooperation; counter-trade, etc.

Another agreement which was signed between the two countries in 1993 was the Agreement on Avoidance of Double Taxation. In May 1999, an agreement on Bilateral Investment Promotion and Protection was also signed. The IGC (Inter-Governmental Commission) has met nine times and the last Session was held in Tashkent on May 4, 2011.

Bilateral Trade

According to Uzbekistan State Committee for Statistics, Uzbekistan's imports from India increased from US$79.9 million in 2008 to US$163.4 in 2012. The country's exports to India also increased from US$11.1 million in 2008 to US$37.82 million in 2012.

Uzbekistan imports several items from India, such as drugs, pharmaceutical products, paper, wood products, machinery, garments & fabrics, tea, plastic items, chemicals, surgical items and consumer goods.

On the other hand, Uzbekistan exports to India include beans, chemicals, non-ferrous metals, machinery, silver, raw cotton & silk, pulses & services.

Uzbekistan was the first country that Modi visited during his five-nation tour of Central Asia. Recent years have witnessed building up of a strategic partnership on the foundation of mutual respect and shared interests between the two countries, which encompasses expanding economic cooperation, combating terrorism, advancing stability in the region and promoting regional integration.

The Prime Minister, Shri Narendra Modi paying tribute at the bust of the former Prime Minister, Shri Lal Bahadur Shastri in Tashkent, Uzbekistan on July 07, 2015.

Modi on meeting with the Uzbek President, Islam Karimov, said, "*It reflects our resolve to start a new era in our relations with Central Asian Republics. Our relationship with the region has ancient roots and has left a strong imprint on both. It now occupies a significant place in India's future.*"

Both the leaders agreed to raise the level of bilateral economic engagement. Modi conveyed the strong business interest elicited by the Indian business community for investing in Uzbekistan.

Investment Opportunities

Modi unfolded his 'inclusive economic agenda' and 'Make in India' initiative in Uzbekistan and said, "*There is immense potential for investment in a broad range of areas in Uzbekistan.*" However, he appealed to Uzbekistan government to smoothen the process and make its policies investment-friendly for Indian investments in the country.

The Prime Minister, Shri Narendra Modi releasing the first Uzbek-Hindi dictionary along with the Prime Minister of Uzbekistan, Mr. Shavkat Miromonovich Mirziyoyev and the Indologist Rakhmatov in Tashkent, Uzbekistan on July 07, 2015.

Supply of Uranium

President Karimov expressed his support for strengthening the ongoing cooperation in the areas of agriculture, information technology and energy. In turn, Modi is believed to have stressed on the need to implement the contract signed earlier between the two countries for supply of uranium from this uranium-rich country.

Connectivity

Need to enhance connectivity between the two countries was expressed by the two leaders, who discussed various initiatives to be taken in this area. Modi explained and proposed membership of the International North South Transport Corridor to Uzbekistan and also sought President Karimov's support to India in joining the Ashgabat Agreement.

In an attempt to bring the people of the two countries together in the areas of culture and tourism, Modi appealed for addressing the need for enhancing people-to-people contact. He praised Uzbekistan for being the forerunner in nurturing Hindi and Indian culture on its soil.

Modi welcomed President Karimov's assurance for speedy completion of the Entrepreneurship Development Centre at Tashkent and said that India will expand cooperation in capacity building through increase in the number of training opportunities in India. India's commitment saw the upgradation of the Uzbekistan-India Information Technology Centre in 2015.

Defence and Cyber Security

The two leaders discussed regional and international issues, including the situation in Afghanistan and together expressed concern on the rising threat of extremism and terrorism in their 'extended neighbourhood'. The two sides decided to intensify security cooperation and step up exchanges in this area. The 'Bilateral Joint Working Group on Counter Terrorism' was also scheduled to meet later in 2015. Strengthening cooperation in defence and cyber security was also agreed upon by the two sides.

The two sides also decided to work together within the framework of the Shanghai Cooperation Organisation.

Indian Diaspora

While in Uzbekistan, Modi interacted with the Indologists in Tashkent and mingled with Hindi language students and Indian community members there. He took time out to pay tribute to former Indian Prime Minister Lal Bahadur Shastri at his memorial in Tashkent and thanked the people of Tashkent and Uzbekistan for preserving the legacy of India's former Prime Minister. The Lal Bahadur Shastri Centre for Indian Culture, under ICCR (Indian Council for Cultural Relations), was established in Tashkent in 1995 and has been a household name in Uzbekistan for its cultural activities.

The Centre for Indian Culture besides organising seminar events related to Indian culture also organises regular classes in Indian classical dance, Kathak and also for yoga. It also promotes the Hindi language, in addition to six Uzbek educational institutions that promote studies of Indian languages, particularly Hindi, from primary to post-graduate level, nationwide. During his stay, Modi also visited the Monument of Independence and Humanism.

The year 1996 saw the setting up of the India Chair at Tashkent at the University of World Economy and Diplomacy and in 2012 Uzbek Radio completed 50 years of Hindi broadcasting. In addition, the Indian serials of *Ramayana* and *Mahabharata* have been telecast more than once by the Uzbek TV channels.

Protocol for Cooperation in the field of information and mass media envisages exchange of TV programmes, visit of journalists, participation in international film festivals, cooperation among the filmmakers of both feature films and documentaries, visit of Radio and TV personnel etc. This protocol was initially signed in October 1992 between India and Uzbekistan and was subsequently rejuvenated with a similar protocol in May 2000 during the visit of President Islam Karimov to India.

The Prime Minister, Shri Narendra Modi shaking hands with the President of Uzbekistan, Mr. Islam Karimov, after the Joint Press Statement at Kuksaroy Complex in Tashkent, Uzbekistan on July 06, 2015.

Since 1993-94, Uzbekistan continues to be a beneficiary of India's ITEC (Indian Technical and Economic Cooperation) Programme that currently allots 150 slots annually. This Programme that has several areas of training, including information technology, English language, management, journalism, diplomacy, small business planning, remote sensing, banking and hotel management etc. has been very well received in Uzbekistan.

It is to the credit of ITEC that Uzbek students utilised all the allotted slots during the last three years from 2010-13. The ICCR's Scholarship Programmes also offers 20 scholarships annually to Uzbekistan for various courses in the Indian Universities.

Modi in KAZAKHSTAN (July 7 to 8, 2015)

"Kazakhstan is one of the few countries with ample capacity to expand oil production. This makes them very important to maintain global energy balances." —**Ricardo Hausmann**, Professor, Harvard University

India-Kazakhstan Relations

India continues to enjoy warm and friendly relations with Kazakhstan. The bilateral relations between Astana and Delhi based on equal partnership, mutual respect and understanding continue to mature from year to year. These ties show great potential to raise Kazakhstan-India relations to a new level of cooperation.

There are several similarities between both countries; since both are multi-ethnic, multi-linguistic, multi-cultural societies. They are committed to following secular policies and countering fundamentalism, religious extremism and terrorism. Kazakhstan respects and recognises India's global and regional standing and its views coincide with India's on all major domestic and international issues.

The Prime Minister, Shri Narendra Modi shaking hands with the President of the Republic of Kazakhstan, Mr. Nursultan Nazarbayev after the Joint Press Statement, at Akorda President's Palace, in Astana, Kazakhstan on July 08, 2015.

It was only two decades ago that India established its diplomatic relations with Kazakhstan, although there have been continued exchanges between the two countries since the days of the Great Silk Road. In February 22, 1992, an agreement which was signed between the two countries, formalised the close friendly relations between the two based on the fundamental principles of international cooperation. In February 1992, just after Kazakhstan regained independence, President Nazarbayev chose India as the first country to visit outside the CIS. In reciprocation, the then Prime Minister Narasimha Rao visited Kazakhstan in 1993.

The Prime Minister, Shri Narendra Modi with the Prime Minister of the Republic of Kazakhstan, Mr. Karim Massimov in the round-table interaction with the CEOs and business leaders of Kazakhstan and India in Astana, Kazakhstan on July 07, 2015.

More recently, President Nazarbayev paid a State visit to India in January 2009, when he was invited as the Chief Guest on India's 60th Republic Day celebrations. He gave significant impetus to the ties between the two countries. This initiative also made Kazakhstan a key element of India's proclaimed 'Extended Neighborhood' and 'Connect Central Asia' policies.

Modi's Visit to Kazakhstan

Prime Minister Modi began his tour of Kazakhstan on an emotive note describing the nation as that of global stature and respect. He lauded the progress made by the country in the past 10 years, thus, *"This is not just because Mother Nature has been generous to you with resources of every kind, it is because of your investment in education, human resources and infrastructure that have helped increase the size of your economy four times in the last 10 years."*

The Prime Minister, Shri Narendra Modi in the round-table interaction with the CEOs and business leaders of Kazakhstan and India, in Astana, Kazakhstan on July 07, 2015. The Prime Minister of the Republic of Kazakhstan, Mr. Karim Massimov is also seen.

Modi also praised Kazakh leadership for advancing peace and cooperation in the great Eurasian region and said, "*Kazakhstan is a voice of responsibility and maturity in international forums, including the United Nations. No Indian will forget Kazakhstan's generosity in making way for India's bid for the membership of the UN Security Council in 2011-12.*"

Modi was invited to the Akorda Presidential Palace in Astana where he held talks on various issues with Kazakh President Nursultan Nazarbayev. The two leaders agreed to focus on boosting trade, energy, defence and security cooperation. This resulted in inking five agreements, in defence, railways, uranium supply, sports and transfer of sentenced prisoners.

Modi declared Kazakhstan as India's biggest economic partner in Central Asia, but accepted the fact that the economic ties between the two have been modest. He said, "*We will work together to take economic ties to a new level.*" India took the opportunity to purchase uranium from Kazakhstan, the world's largest producer of the mineral, by inking a "*much larger second contract*". On cooperation in the hydrocarbons sector, PM Modi said, "*Mr. Nazarbayev responded positively to my request to consider additional mature blocks for Indian investments.*"

Both sides agreed to give priority to investment in manufacturing and infrastructure and also boost cooperation in renewable energy. Modi said, "*India will participate on a large scale in the Expo 2017 in Astana.*"

The two sides also agreed to enhance cooperation in space and information technology and also boost connectivity through the International North-South Transport Corridor, the Iran-Turkmenistan-Kazakhstan rail link and Chabahar port in Iran.

A new youth exchange programme with six Kazakh universities was finalised for the next five years between the two countries.

On defence and security, Modi remarked, "*Our defence and security cooperation is an important dimension of our strategic partnership. We both want to make it stronger, including in defence manufacturing. We welcome the new Memorandum of Understanding on defence cooperation.*"

Touching upon India's bid for a permanent seat in a reformed United Nations Security Council and for a UN Comprehensive Convention on International Terrorism, Modi thanked Kazakhstan's President for continued support for India's candidature and assured him of India's support for Kazakhstan's candidature for a non-permanent seat in the UNSC for 2017-18.

The Prime Minister, Shri Narendra Modi being welcomed on his arrival at Astana International Airport, Kazakhstan on July 07, 2015.

The joint statement, termed as Tej Kadam, quoted the two leaders' stress on the importance of a stable and secure environment for peaceful economic development in view of the rising challenge posed by terrorism in many parts of the world and in their immediate region. They also underlined the importance of a stable and secure environment for peaceful economic development and agreed to continue their fight against terrorism and extremism including exchange of information regarding the same. In this context, both laid emphasis on the importance of regular inter-agency consultations and meetings of the Joint Working Group on Counter-Terrorism and also called for early conclusion of the UN Comprehensive Convention on International Terrorism.

The signing of agreement on defence and military-technical cooperation which would further widen the scope of bilateral defence cooperation including regular exchange of visits, consultations, training of military personnel, military-technical cooperation, joint exercises, special forces exchanges and cooperation in the area of UN peacekeeping operations was welcomed by the two leaders.

An MoU, deemed the 'roadmap' on trade, economic and investment cooperation, which would identify concrete projects in various sectors and assist in efficient implementation of projects in both the countries to activate bilateral trade and economic relations, was signed between JSC Kazxnex Invest of Kazakhstan and the Indian JSC Invest India.

Welcoming the establishment of a Joint Study Group between India and the Eurasian Economic Union on the feasibility of a FTA (Free Trade Agreement) both leaders were confident that it would boost trade.

To improve surface connectivity for trade with Kazakhstan, the two sides agreed to set up a dedicated freight terminal in one of the western seaports of India. Both the leaders were confident that these initiatives, including the International North-South Transport Corridor, will serve to enhance economic and commercial interaction between the two countries in the future. The two sides welcomed signing of the MOU on Technical Cooperation in railways between the NC Kazakhstan Temir Zholy JSC and India's railways ministry.

Modi in TURKMENISTAN (July 10-11, 2015)

"Cooperation, confidence and mutual respect are the principles that lie in the basis of international activity of Turkmenistan." —**Gurbanguly Berdimuhamedow**, President of Turkmenistan

The relations between India and Turkmenistan had been historically and culturally deep-rooted, as the two countries continue to share interest in international as well as regional peace and stability. So, it was no surprise that President Gurbanguly Berdimuhamedow of Turkmenistan extended an invitation to Modi to visit his country.

As a result, Modi scheduled a two-day State visit to the country on July 10 and 11, 2015. The two leaders took the opportunity to hold extensive discussions on bilateral relations as well as regional and international issues of mutual interest.

The two leaders agreed to boost regular bilateral interactions at all levels and in all bilateral and multilateral events, as a positive outcome of increased high-level exchanges between the two countries in recent years.

On the successful conclusion of the 5th Meeting of the Turkmen-India Inter-Governmental Joint Commission on trade, economic, scientific and technological cooperation, held in Ashgabat on April 8, 2015, the two leaders acknowledged the new and potential areas of cooperation that the Commission had identified. The two not only called for effective implementation of the decisions made at the meeting, but also stressed the need to strengthen other institutional linkages.

They also expressed the desire to hold regular dialogue on bilateral, regional and global issues by their senior officials on mutually agreed issues through the existing mechanisms, such as Foreign Office Consultations, Consular Consultations, Joint Working Group on Energy as well as establishment of additional mechanisms.

Modi expressed his desire for early implementation of the US$10 billion TAPI pipeline project and conveyed India's interest in long-term investment in the energy sector in Turkmenistan. During the visit, the two countries signed seven pacts. The pacts included an agreement on cooperation in the field of defence and one on tourism.

Prime Minister, Shri Narendra Modi being welcomed on his arrival at Ashgabat International Airport, Turkmenistan on July 10, 2015.

The two leaders promised to jointly combat terrorism, organised crime and illegal drug-trafficking in the region. Identifying terrorism as a major threat facing the region, Modi said, "*We have shared interest in a peaceful and stable Afghanistan and Central Asia. We have also common purpose in combating terrorism and extremism in our region.*"

Touching upon TAPI (Turkmenistan-Afghanistan-Pakistan-India) project, Modi termed it as a significant relation-building initiative between the two countries and conveyed his eagerness to explore the possibility of land-sea route through Iran for the pipeline. This would facilitate Turkmenistan, which holds the world's fourth-largest natural gas reserves, to pump gas to India and Pakistan, through Afghanistan. On the TAPI project, Berdymukhamedov had this to say, "*We are standing on the threshold of a remarkable event that would create 12,000 new jobs in Afghanistan. Apart from the economic rationale for all the participants in the project, TAPI is aimed at making a large contribution to strengthening stability in the region.*"

The Prime Minister, Shri Narendra Modi witnesses the practice of Yoga, at the inauguration of the Traditional Medicine and Yoga Centre, in Ashgabat, Turkmenistan on July 11, 2015.

The Prime Minister, Shri Narendra Modi paid tributes at the bust of the Mahatma Gandhi, at the Bagtyarlyk Sports Complex, in Ashgabat, Turkmenistan on July 11, 2015.

The two leaders acknowledged TAPI as a 'key pillar' of economic engagement between the two countries and concurred that implementing it would have a transformational impact on trade. To this end, both the leaders agreed to finalise TAPI's Consortium Leader by September 1, 2015. Expressing their strong commitment towards timely implementation, Modi also expressed India's readiness for long-term investment in Turkmenistan in the energy sector. Terming connectivity as a key aspect of the relationship, Modi expressed the need for enhancing it and proposed that Turkmenistan be a part of International North South Transport Corridor.

According to Modi, a "*positive discussion*" had ensued with Berdimuhamedow on India's interest in investment in downstream industries, including petrochemicals and fertiliser. This resulted in MoU that will enable long term arrangements for supply of fertilisers from Turkmenistan to India.

Touching upon defence, Modi was of the opinion that a defence pact would build a framework for intensifying bilateral defence and security cooperation by high and mid-level visits between the two countries. In addition, training and dialogue between the Ministries of Defence and other relevant organisations will also contribute to this cause, enabling capacity-building and technical cooperation.

Congratulating Berdimuhamedow on the 20th anniversary of policy of Permanent Neutrality that promotes peace and stability in the wider region, Modi stressed the need for greater cooperation in the energy sector. He welcomed the decision of ONGC Videsh Limited to open an office in Ashgabat and said, *"We had a very positive discussion on India's interest in investment in downstream industries, including petrochemicals and fertiliser."*

Lauding Turkmenistan for supporting India to join the Ashgabat Agreement on trade and transit, Modi remarked, *"If we use the Iran route, Ashgabat is the first capital we would reach in Central Asia. Together with the Kazakhstan-Turkmenistan-Iran rail link, and India's proposed investment in Chahbahar Port in Iran, these initiatives will strengthen connectivity between our countries. As India deepens its relations with Central Asia, Turkmenistan will play a crucial role in it."*

To streamline movement of goods and commodities between India and Turkmenistan and beyond, Modi was upbeat about the recently inaugurated three-nation railway line that could act as a linked corridor of the International North South Transport Corridor. India's proposal to set up a urea production facility in Turkmenistan was welcomed by the two leaders.

It was only apt for Modi to present a specially handcrafted horse saddle to President Berdimuhamedow, who is a keen horse rider and known for his passion for horse breeding, racing and equestrian. He also thanked Berdimuhamedow for supporting

June 21 as IDY (International Day of Yoga) at the United Nations and for the "*extensive celebrations*" of the first IDY in Ashgabat. Two MoUs signed between the two countries included one on cooperation in yoga and traditional medicine and the other on sports.

Defence and Security Cooperation

The two leaders decided to enhance their cooperation in countering various security threats, including cross-border terrorism, organised crime and illegal drug trafficking. To this end, the two welcomed the signing of the Defence Cooperation Agreement that provides a framework for intensifying bilateral defence and security cooperation and capacity building and technical cooperation in the defence sector.

Economic Engagement

Identifying energy, petrochemicals, transport, communications, information and technology, textile industry, chemical and pharmaceutical industry, construction and agro-processing as potential areas for cooperation between the two countries, the two leaders felt the need to increase trade manifold for the mutual benefit of both countries. They also promoted participation of private companies of both countries by agreeing to create favourable conditions for it.

The need to hold exhibitions, business forums and other trade events in both the countries was emphasised by the two leaders for facilitating business interactions and linkages between the two.

Energy and Petrochemicals

The two leaders welcomed establishment of 'TAPI Ltd' as a Special Purpose Vehicle (SPV) in November 2014 in Ashgabat and acknowledged that it was a milestone in implementation of this strategic project. They also welcomed the opening of OVL (ONGC Videsh Ltd.) representative office in Turkmenistan and MOU between the State Concern 'Turkmenhimiya' and Indian PSU (Public Sector Undertaking), Rashtriya Chemicals and Fertilisers Limited for long-term sourcing of urea from Turkmenistan.

Transport and Connectivity

Visualising the need for exploring alternative transport corridors for additional connectivity options between the two countries, the two leaders welcomed the first expert level meeting on connectivity between India and Turkmenistan in Delhi in June 2015. They agreed on a JWG for exploring various connectivity options between India and Turkmenistan. India's intention to join the Ashgabat Agreement won support from the President of Turkmenistan.

The significance of Turkmenistan as a gateway to other Central Asian countries and the Caspian region was acknowledged by the two leaders, who agreed to support each other's initiatives to facilitate movement of goods through INSTC (International North South Transport Corridor). The President of Turkmenistan expressed their desire to become party to this Corridor. Modi visualized the recently inaugurated Kazakhstan-Turkmenistan-Iran railway line as a linked corridor of the INSTC to streamline movement of goods.

The two leaders called for increasing frequency of flight operations between the two countries, including by offering fifth freedom rights for increased viability. They agreed to implement suitable measures to encourage transportation of cargo through their respective airlines.

The Prime Minister, Shri Narendra Modi with the President of Turkmenistan, Mr. Gurbanguly Berdimuhamedow at the Ceremonial Welcome, at Independence Square, in Oguzkhan Palace, Ashgabat, Turkmenistan on July 11, 2015.

Capacity Building and Science & Technology

The leaders lauded the role of ITEC programme that has helped Turkmen nationals in capacity building and human resource development and in creating a talented pool of professionals in the country for meeting developmental needs across various sectors. Modi further promised India's willingness to offer new training courses to Turkmenistan in the desired sectors and was appreciated by the President of Turkmenistan for this proposal.

The two leaders welcomed the successful upgradation of the India-Turkmenistan Industrial Training Centre in Ashgabat and also welcomed the signing of the Programme of Cooperation in Science and Technology.

Cultural Cooperation

For deepening the bonds of friendship and mutual understanding between the peoples of the two countries, the two leaders underlined the importance of cultural exchanges. They noted the successful holding of Turkmen cultural festival in India in 2014 and ICCR 'Namaste Turkmenistan' festival in various parts of Turkmenistan in 2015. They called for similar events to be held in future as well.

To this end the two leaders agreed to finalise the Programme of Cooperation on Culture between the two countries and also acknowledged the stronger bonds with Turkmen students through scholarships offered by ICCR.

The strengthening of cultural ties through the inauguration of a Centre of Yoga and Traditional Medicine in Ashgabat was acknowledged by both the leaders, who underscored the universal value of Yoga and its positive and holistic perspective on health. Modi thanked President Berdimuhamedow for declaring June 21 as International Day of Yoga (IDY) at the United Nations and for the extensive celebrations of the first IDY in Ashgabat.

The topic of conducting the 5th Asian Indoor and Martial Arts Games in Ashgabat in 2017 was touched by the two sides and both leaders promised to work towards making it a success.

The bust of Mahatma Gandhi was unveiled in Ashgabat that symbolised the commitment of both countries to work together towards a peaceful world order.

International Cooperation

The two leaders underscored the need for enhancing the role of the United Nations and its institutions in addressing global issues and safeguarding sustainable development. Congratulating the President of Turkmenistan on the 20th anniversary of adoption of Permanent Neutrality at the United Nations, Modi acknowledged the contribution of this policy to peace, development and stability in Turkmenistan and the region at large.

The need to reform the United Nations Security Council for strengthening and expanding its role in addressing the pressing contemporary challenges was acknowledged by the two leaders. The two promised to maintain close interaction and coordination in order to create a favourable international environment for the development of the two countries within the UN framework.

Looking Ahead

The President of Turkmenistan acknowledged that Modi's visit has helped in consolidating the longstanding cordial relations between the two countries. The two leaders promised to work closely on issues discussed and agreed during their official talks and enhance mutually beneficial partnership. On his part, Modi invited the President of Turkmenistan to India at a date and time of his convenience, which the latter graciously accepted.

Modi in TAJIKISTAN (July 11-12, 2015)

"The vision of Mawlana Hazar Imam that diversity of humankind is a gift of God. And that pluralism in Islam a blessing rather than a burden is of great value, which needs to be supported and understood." —**Emomali Rahmon**, President of Tajikistan

Prime Minister Narendra Modi arrived in Tajikistan on the last leg of his week-long tour of five Central Asian countries and held wide ranging talks with Tajikistan President Emomali Rahmon on bilateral, regional and international issues.

A joint statement issued after the meeting said that the two leaders underlined the importance of a stable and secure environment for economic development and prosperity of their countries and agreed to cooperation in the fight against terrorism and extremism and reaffirmed their determination to act resolutely against organisations and agencies supporting terrorism.

Modi reiterated India's commitment to support the development of Tajikistan's defence capacities for enhancing stability and security, while thanking Tajikistan for supporting India's proposal to declare June 21 as International Day of Yoga in the United Nations and for its membership to SCO.

Expressing happiness on the excellent relations between the two countries, President Rahmon and Prime Minister Modi acknowledged the shared history and cultural affinities between their people. The two leaders envisioned transforming bilateral relations into a multi-faceted strategic partnership for the mutual benefit of both the countries.

The two leaders, while welcoming the continuing exchanges at ministerial and senior official levels with regard to bilateral ties, called for an enhanced focus on the implementation of the outcomes of bilateral agreements and MOUs in various areas.

The Prime Minister, Shri Narendra Modi being welcomed on his arrival at the India-Tajik Friendship Hospital, in Quarghan Teppa, Dushanbe, Tajikistan on July 13, 2015.

Recognising the increased threat to India and Tajikistan due to rising extremism and terrorism in many parts of the world and in their immediate neighbourhood, both the leaders rooted for the adoption of 'Comprehensive Convention on International Terrorism' by the UN General Assembly.

In order to strengthen the cooperation in the fight against terrorism, the two leaders expressed the desire to boost official-level interactions within the framework of JWG (Joint Working

Group) on Counter Terrorism. They wanted the JWG to meet at an early date.

Terming secular governance as common ideal for both the countries, Modi appreciated Tajikistan's efforts on curbing extremism and radicalism to ensure secular governance.

Dubbing defence cooperation as one of the main pillars of partnership between the two countries, Modi assured India's commitment to support the development of Tajikistan's defence capacities to enhance stability and security, which the President of Tajikistan heartily welcomed.

The Prime Minister, Shri Narendra Modi laying wreath at the Ismaili Somoni Monument, at Dusti Square, in Dushanbe, Tajikistan on July 13, 2015.

The Prime Minister, Shri Narendra Modi shaking hands with the President of Tajikistan, Mr. Emomali Rahmon after the Joint Press Briefing, at Qasr-e-Millat, in Dushanbe, Tajikistan on July 13, 2015.

The two leaders acknowledged not exploiting full potential of trade and economic linkages being close neighboring countries and emphasised on the importance of trade and investments to boost economic relations between the two countries. To deepen trade and investment relations and facilitate exchanges between the business communities, the two leaders agreed to hold the 8th session of the India-Tajikistan JCM (Joint Commission on Trade, Economic, Scientific and Technical Cooperation) in Dushanbe in 2015.

Terming connectivity between the two countries as essential to realising the full potential of trade and commerce, the two leaders agreed to explore the possibilities of developing an alternate surface route in cooperation with other countries of the region. Tajikistan extended full support to the International North South Transport Corridor (INSTC) and wanted speedy implementation of the same. This Corridor will not only considerably reduce transit time, but also the cost of transportation of goods between India, Central Asia and beyond.

Modi expressed his desire to be included in the proposed PATTTTA (Pakistan, Afghanistan and Tajikistan Trilateral Transit Trade Agreement) that would facilitate trade between Tajikistan and the countries of the South Asian region. President Rahmon promised further consultations on India's inclusion to this arrangement.

Recognising air connectivity as important for trade and economic linkages as well as tourism and greater people-to-people interactions, the two leaders agreed to find ways and means for increasing the frequency of flights on the Delhi-Dushanbe sector, including the provision of Fifth Freedom rights for carriers.

Tajikistan expressed its desire for agricultural cooperation with India, given India's expertise in this sector, including research, development and processing of agricultural products. Tajikistan also demanded greater involvement of Indian companies in the country's agricultural sector.

Hydropower Cooperation

The President of Tajikistan, while expressing its gratitude to India for successful upgradation and modernisation of the Varzob-1 Hydro Power Station through BHEL (Bharat Heavy Electricals Limited) and NHPC (National Hydroelectric Power Corporation) as well as various training programmes, sought greater Indian involvement in hydropower generation in Tajikistan.

Health Sector

While sharing the common dream of enhanced cooperation in health sector, the President of Tajikistan welcomed India's proposal to implement a tele-medicine project by connecting reputed multi-speciality hospitals in India with hospitals in Dushanbe and other regions of Tajikistan for medical consultation and education.

The Prime Minister, Shri Narendra Modi inspecting the Guard of Honour, during the Ceremonial Reception, at the Qasr-e-Millat, in Dushanbe, Tajikistan on July 13, 2015. The President of Tajikistan, Mr. Emomali Rahmon is also seen.

Bilateral Economic Engagement

Identifying promising areas for further cooperation, such as education, food processing, mining, pharmaceuticals, textiles, skill development, science & technology, information technology, culture and tourism, the leaders underlined the importance of enhancing closer interactions between the business bodies and investment promotion agencies of the two countries.

People-to-People Ties

Terming cultural interactions as important for further strengthening the close bonds between the peoples of the two countries, the two leaders called for active implementation of the Programme of Cooperation between India and Tajikistan on Art and Culture for the period 2016-18 and agreed to organise 'Days of Culture' in each other's country.

Modi appreciated and expressed his gratitude to the President of Tajikistan for installing a bust of the renowned Indian poet, Rabindranath Tagore in Dushanbe. The two were in agreement over the contemporary relevance of Tagore's writings that will help promote harmony between the two cultures.

The huge popularity of Indian cinema in Tajikistan, prompted the two leaders to extend cooperation in the field of television and radio-broadcasting that will promote people-to-people contacts and cultural understanding.

Expressing satisfaction at the admirable cooperation between the two countries on multilateral issues and all out mutual support for their initiatives in the United Nations and other international forums, the two leaders desired to strengthen such interactions on issues of mutual interests to both countries.

In a mutual give and take, the President of Tajikistan reiterated its support for India's candidature for permanent membership of an expanded UN Security Council, while Modi thanked Tajikistan for supporting India's membership to the Shanghai Cooperation Organisation (SCO) established for economic development, security and stability of the region.

Modi in KYRGYSTAN (July 12, 2015)

"Develop internal resources and transform them into internal investments." —**Askar Akayev,** Former President of Kyrgyzstan

Prime Minister Modi began his one-day Kyrgyzstan tour on a positive note, indicating to the country's President Atambayev that his visit would take bilateral cooperation between the two countries to 'new heights'.

The Prime Minister, Shri Narendra Modi addressing the gathering after unveiling the Statute of Mahatma Gandhi, at Mahatma Gandhi Avenue, in Bishkek, Kyrgyzstan on July 12, 2015. The Prime Minister of Kyrgyz Republic, Mr. Temir Sariyev is also seen.

Putting forward his agenda of inclusive economic development and regional cooperation, Modi called for enhanced cooperation between the Central Asian countries and India and said together they could reinforce each other's economic progress and stressed the need for peace and secure neighbourhood to carry out economic progress, while seeking a united action to combat menace like terrorism and extremism.

The Prime Minister, Shri Narendra Modi inaugurating the Tele-medicine link between India and Kyrgyzstan at National Centre for Cardiology & Internal Medicine, in Bishkek, Kyrgyzstan on July 12, 2015. The Prime Minister of Kyrgyz Republic, Mr. Temir Sariyev is also seen.

Modi said, "*The central Asian countries and India can reinforce each other's economic progress as sustainable development is important for both. We can contribute to cooperation and integration across the different regions of Asia.*" He further added, "*My visit to all five countries in the region demonstrates the importance that we attach to a new level of relationship with Central Asia. Kyrgyzstan is a key part of that vision.*"

Modi had an enriching discussion with Kyrgyzstan President Atambayev on strengthening relations between the two countries in trade, investment, tourism, culture and human resource development. Welcoming the agreements on standards and culture, Modi said that the collective initiative between India and Central Asia will boost the economic ties between the two countries.

Modi acknowledged the admirable contribution of President Atambayev to democracy and development and said that he was happy for the agreement on cooperation that India's Election Commissions had signed with Kyrgyzstan. Modi invited Kyrgyz Parliamentary delegation to India after the parliamentary elections in the Kyrgyz Republic.

The Prime Minister, Shri Narendra Modi and the President of Kyrgyz Republic, Mr. Almazbek Atambayev at the signing ceremony, in Ala-Archa State Residence, Bishkek, Kyrgyzstan on July 12, 2015.

Terming launching of tele-medicine link with India as first in the region, Modi expounded the possibilities of the digital world. He also promised to initiate the second phase of the Kyrgyz-India Mountain Bio-Medical Research Centre.

Modi promised to increase the training offers to 100 in 2015 and agreed to enhance India's engagement in capacity building.

Informing about establishing India-Kyrgyz Centre for Information Technology in the Kyrgyz State University in Bishkek, Modi said that Information Technology is critical for success in today's world for creating opportunities for the youth. He promised similar centres in other major cities in Kyrgyzstan.

Stressing upon the importance of agriculture sector for both India and the Kyrgyz Republic, the two leaders vowed to explore possible avenues for cooperation and identify concrete projects in the agriculture sector through a round table conference in Bishkek.

The Prime Minister, Shri Narendra Modi at the Victory Monument, in Victory Square, Bishkek, Kyrgyzstan on July 12, 2015.

Later, Modi unveiled the statue of Mahatma Gandhi on the street that bears his name and said, "*I thank the people of Kyrgyzstan for this honour. His life and message are universal and timeless. This statue will also remind the residents of our shared values.*"

In defence sector, Modi said India and the Kyrgyz Republic have maintained strong defence ties. He further added, "*We have just completed a joint exercise 'Khanjar 2015' and have decided to hold joint military exercises on an annual basis. The IT Centre in the Kyrgyz Military Academy is an example of innovative cooperation that is important to both the countries.*"

Modi expressed his confidence that the new agreement on defence cooperation between the two countries would provide a framework to broaden their engagement by the inclusion of defence technology.

Modi congratulated President Atambayev for joining EEU (Eurasian Economic Union) and said that a Free Trade Agreement between India and EEU will substantially increase the cooperation between the two countries. He envisioned making Kyrgyzstan a base for India's economic engagement in the region.

Modi expressed his gratitude to President Atambayev for his strong support to India's candidature for permanent membership of an expanded United Nations Security Council and also for endorsing the International Day of Yoga on June 21.

CHAPTER 9

ON THE HOME TURF – THE ROAD AHEAD

"Without strategy, execution is aimless. Without execution, strategy is useless." – **Morris Chang**

During the nineties, when our nation was passing through the phase of liberalisation, the state that developed the most was Gujarat. It actually surprised many by its course of development. Its excellent performance was the result of a proficient administration and a business friendly environment. However, this all could be achieved because of the dynamic and visionary leadership of its then Chief Minister – Narendra Damodar Modi. By transforming the government departments into efficient and cohesive machinery, eager to reach out to the expectations of the industry, Modi made the state of Gujarat a paradise for investors!

Thus, it was not at all surprising that companies from all over India looked upon Gujarat to set up industries. So much so, companies from Maharashtra, a fully developed industrial state, too joined in the foray. Such was the charisma of Narendra Bhai Modi! When the Tata Motors was forced to leave West Bengal, Modi was quick to seize on the opportunity. Gujarat thus provided the fumbling Tata Motors with the best of facilities and support. This had a profound effect on the business community at large. In view of such initiatives many large companies felt obliged to put up their industries there. Modi called this 'the Gujarat Model'. Excellent infrastructure, controlled bureaucracy and business friendly environment were some of the salient features of this framework that soon became the talk of the nation.

This was not bereft of political connotations as it was soon to reap in rich dividends for Modi's party – the BJP (Bharatiya Janata Party). Modi himself became synonym for growth and development. Come Lok Sabha Elections, Modi was projected as the Prime Minister Candidate and people across class, caste and creed, and even political parties voted him to power! They counted on him and saw in him a person capable of delivering. He came to power with a general belief that 'good days are ahead' – there would be industrialisation all across the nation with opportunities for all. True to his promise, Modi did get down to work as soon as he took over the charge.

While conceptualising the 'Make in India' program Prime Minister Modi believed that if foreign investment would pour in, the country would prosper at a faster pace. Therefore he visited several countries to lure in investors. Investors too were highly impressed by his overall work culture and efficient dialogue and believed him while he promised to do all he could to weed out obstacles that came into the way of setting up of industries in India. It may be recalled that the foreign investors were wary of the tax regime in India. Modi assured them that the rules and laws would be simplified.

All these efforts are sure to get rewards in due course. During his two visits to the USA, he met the CEOs (Chief Executive Officers) and Chairmen of several corporate and business houses, who spelt out their commitment to invest in India. As per the news from the United States, almost US$ 410 million would be invested in India in the course of three years. Companies such as GE (General Electric), Boeing and Westinghouse have showed their interest in setting up their plants in India. China too welcomed PM Modi and assured India of heavy investments to improve upon its infrastructure.

During his visit to Japan, Modi was assured of million dollars' investment in the field of healthcare, foundry, electronics, infrastructure and green energy. The bullet train project has also been committed by Japan. France too has assured India to invest about €2 billion that is exclusive of the Airbus promise. Similar assurances have come from Australia and Canada too. All this certainly presents a healthy picture for the PM's 'Make in India' initiative. This will boost industrialisation.

Yet it may not be a good idea to cave in to the caboodle of large industries. Although it is true that large industries give impetus to economy, yet it may not be completely so in the Indian context. India must appreciate the fact that in terms of its social fabric and geographical variance, India is much different from the developed nations. If it has sailed through, it is because of its small and medium industries, including the cottage industries. It is difficult to have large industries in all states. So, if large industries are not there in all parts of the country, it is not surprising. MSMEs remain the backbone of many Indian states and provide immense job opportunities for its people. Ngozi Okonjo-Iweala (2014) argued that world over two things are important these days, inequality and employment be it in Nigeria, Brazil, USA, UK, Canada, Belgium, South Korea and of course in India. In fact, SME is the answer to tackle these issues. In terms of employment generation, the small scale industries sector is second only to the agriculture sector in India. Unfortunately, both these sectors are in want of some immediate attention.

Here it would be interesting to note that about 40 per cent of the products in the country originate from the unorganised small and medium scale industries sector. The beauty of this sector is that it generates large job opportunities with very little of capital investment. For example, with a capital investment of about hundred-thousand rupees, it may employ as many as four persons. According to ASSOCHAM (Associated Chambers of Commerce of India), the MSMEs engage about 80 million men and women, who produce almost six thousand different kinds of items in more than 31 million units spread across the length and breadth of the country. Even as it remains unorganised, it has been giving boost to Indian economy and has helped the nation surge ahead while running into many slowdowns.

It is wrong to believe that this sector produces only traditional articles. In fact, it also caters to the various needs of large industries. Thus, its products not just go into the market for general buyers, but also find its way to the large industries. MSMEs have indeed helped the nation become self-reliant. These sectors could truly be called poor-friendly as these are labour intensive, rather than machine intensive. Since these industries utilise more hand power than the large industries, they employ more people than the large industries. Furthermore, the MSMEs account for about 8.72 per cent of our GDP (Gross Domestic Product).

It is well known that the large industries need huge infrastructure. Thus, Gujarat, Maharashtra, and Tamil Nadu to some extent, which have successfully built huge infrastructure over the years, have the highest concentration of such industries. This has created an economic imbalance within the country. Moreover, these industries have brought about an influx of labour force thereby making the industrial areas overburdened with population. Had it not been for the small and medium industries that are spread over small towns and cities or in suburbs, India would be witnessing an imbalance of population ratio.

The contribution of MSMEs towards export is also highly commendable. The small and traditional industries account for a major share in export, almost 40 per cent of India's total export. In fact their contribution towards export is more than the large industries.

It may be recalled that in 1991 India had to succumb to certain pressures from the IMF and the World Bank that actually harmed the Indian MSMEs. It was the time when the giant of globalization cast its shadow over Indian small and medium industries. The Indian goods were overshadowed by the cheap foreign goods. The traditional toys industries and the electric goods industries suffered the most. While the foreign goods swept the domestic market, traditional craftsmen were forced to retire. In fact many of them had to retort to selling Chinese goods that had brought them misfortune. This was the only way that they could survive. People employed gainfully in the small scale industries found themselves unemployed now. Gloom fell over traditional craftsmen and they had to abandon their homes in search of new opportunities.

A host of problems still plagues the MSME sector. First and foremost is the lack of finance. In fact, all other problems could said to be emanating from this. Addressing this critical problem Modi has come out with the Pradhan Mantri Mudra Yojna aimed at 'funding the unfunded'. Although the MUDRA Scheme was launched by him with the hope that it would instill new confidence in small entrepreneurs, it has yet to be implemented successfully, in full swing.

Organising collateral security remains a major problem despite various industry associations signing MoUs with commercial banks and other financial institutions to offer collateral security to upcoming entrepreneurs for their credit requirements. 'Via-via-via scheme is not a good idea; it is more of a 'Catch 22' situation. Schemes should be simplified and not become like a spider's web. Adam Lashinsky (2014) remarked that the growth scheme should be frustration free and without complexity. For a loan of say Rs.10,000, small entrepreneurs are forced to mortgage property worth Rs.20,000. Isn't this 'Collateral Terrorism'? in other instances, houses are preferred by banks as collaterals.

There should be clear directions to the banks that houses should not be taken as collaterals. This amounts to punitive measures to safeguard lender's interest.

Besides high cost of credit and irregular availability of raw material, lack of skilled manpower, inadequacy of infrastructural facilities, and poor adaptability to changing trends also prove to be the stumbling blocks. These days SMEs are run by well qualified technical professionals. The MSMEs have better research potential. Most often the government funds for R&D are lost in lengthy and incoherent procedures. Largely the schemes in India to fund R&D activities follow 'via-via-via' route, since MSMEs have no organisation to tackle such a limitless loop for follow up, it culminates in a frustrated end.

There are a few essential steps that the government should consider for the benefit of MSMEs, such as tax exemption for importing samples, prototypes and research/ test equipment. The MSMEs should be insulated from the volatile FE (Foreign Exchange) fluctuation in their transactions. They should be granted loan on the basis of project strength and not on the basis of the promoter's financial strength (especially in residential, real estate, etc.). This sector could be involved in a larger way in CSR (Corporate Social Responsibility). Liberal tax rebates could be provided to them in spending on CSR. Since small industries are widespread, covering a larger area of the country, the nation would be benefitted, if they are involved more in CSR activities. Even the investment allowance should be increased for both MSMEs and large scale industries. Furthermore, small industries should not be used as only outsourcing units for big companies, especially in defence, railways and aerospace industries, but should be integrated into the manufacturing loop.

India has realised the importance of manpower development and have instituted a new ministry dedicated to it. This would prove a boon for our sagging small and medium sector industries and would infuse it with new life. Much is to be done on the technology front though. Marc Benioff (2015) explained that one of the important tricks is to inspire, attract and retain the worthy human asset that leads to culture of innovation. In India, there is a need to develop a strong culture of innovation collectively by government, SMEs and large industries. Brain drain can be stopped by creating the culture of innovation.

It may be recalled that while inaugurating the Vibrant Gujarat Global Investors Summit in 2013, the then Chief Minister Modi had termed MSMEs 'the backbone of economic development'. He had attributed the success of the manufacturing sector in the state to the SMEs. He also made it known that this did not happen with the drop of a hat. A lot of effort had to be put up to encourage the SMEs and clear the hurdles that fell on the way to its success. Remarkably, a growth rate of about 85 per cent was achieved by the small scale industry sector in Gujarat, which was phenomenally higher than the national growth rate of merely 19 per cent shown by this sector. This paved way for the massive industrial growth in the state.

It is very important to have an atmosphere of respect for the people in trade and industry in India. The case in countries like Japan, South Korea, UK, etc. is much different. There the businessmen are considered partners in progress and government officials actually visit them for their opinions and suggestions. Business community is considered the most respected class of people and businesspersons are termed 'engines of growth'.

To exemplify, when South Korea was passing through a critical phase economically, it took a huge loan form the IMF. In order to help the nation repay this loan, the South Korean bank officials visited those people who had taken loans from their banks. In one instance, a banker visited a cobbler who had taken a minor loan and asked him in a helpful manner whether he should increase his earning, thereby enabling him to repay the loan faster. He even offered to relocate the cobbler for bettering his business! The incident displays the concern of the Korean countrymen, who got together to generate the money to repay the IMF loan. This kind of approach should be adopted in India. This is the need of the hour.

Even while industry is a big employment generator, Indian economy is largely based on agriculture and allied business. India cannot borrow 'successful models' from other countries and must note that all such initiatives, to follow the so-called successful models from the West, have failed in this country in the past. Thus, models have to be evolved from within. There is hardly any strife between the farmers and the business community in India. If the farmers progress and have sufficient buying power, business too would prosper. Similarly, prosperity for the Dalit and backward classes segments of the society will help extend the market further. Therefore, this is an encouraging scenario for the business community. Alan Murray (2014) said that for sustainable growth, public should be free and market should also be free. In fact, large corporation also depend on goodwill of the public if they have to survive or thrive on long term.

Interestingly, the farmers as well as the small entrepreneurs have now been equipped with credit cards – the Kissan Credit Card and the Mudra Card. This has merits and demerits of its own, given the socio-economic conditions prevalent in India. Credit Cards cannot be a substitute for cash in hand. Moreover, the world just saw the folly of cashless transactions with enhanced credit limits that almost crippled the US economy. Freedom of choice should be given to the citizens, but government should keep a watch out for 'cash financing terrorism'. In ultimate analysis, the monetary social fabric of India be maintained, while modernising the mechanism and utilizing technology.

It is pertinent to point out that the income should, on an average, be evenly distributed. The prosperity mantra is that liquid money should be in the hands of the people all across the country, be it in agriculture, manufacturing, industry, medicine, education, IT, construction or any other sector. This should be a long-term objective while preparing any kind of regulation.

The country can be sure that PM Modi is also aware of the pitfalls that could block the path of his 'Make in India' initiative. Today the 'Make in India' program is at loggerheads with the 'Made in China' drive that has already gained momentum. In fact, soon after Modi pitched the idea of 'Make in India', the Chinese Premier Li Keqiang announced the 'Made in China' campaign with a host of tax concessions. On the other hand, foreign investors are still sceptic towards India's bureaucratic approach, tax regulations, unconducive labour laws, GST and land reforms.

There is also the need to redefine MSMEs. As of now, any enterprise that employs fewer than ten persons and does not exceed an investment of Rs.2.5 million is a Micro Enterprise. No sooner than it has more than 10 employees, but remains restricted to 50, and invests Rs.2.5 million to Rs.50 million, it is categorised as a Small Enterprise. Medium Enterprises are such units that have fewer than 250 employees and have investments in plant and machinery worth Rs.50 million to Rs.100 million. For Service Enterprises the investments are even lower. Such limitations are unrealistic and are a hindrance to the growth of this sector. In fact, these are inhibiting the growth to the small industries. To highlight the inadequacy of Rs.100 million, consider this: three good CNC (Computerised Numerically Controlled) machines and allied tools cost around US$2 million and one PCB (Printed Circuit Board) mounted assembly line (even without marking boards) cost approximately US$2 million. It means, these limits should be liberally and practically revised. For example, medium scale investment limit should be equal to at least US$10 million and there should be a mechanism to upgrade this limit every year.

Keeping the larger interest in mind, that is, employment and revenue generation, adequate motivation should be provided to this sector. In fact, this sector should be given sizeable tax exemptions on income, R&D and services. Upliftment of this segment of industry in the country could be a game changer and remove inequality. Christine Lagarde (2014) maintains that inequality does not provide sustainable growth moreover it enhances the risk of financial system. Inequality can be best tackled by creating the job for everyone. She further states that income should not be taxed excessively as it provides disincentive to perform and make growth.

Many government departments and agencies are actually working on the problems being faced by SMEs. However, their pace is very slow. All such endeavours need to be more coordinated and more focused. The strengthening of MSMEs in India is of paramount importance to the country besides bringing in foreign investments into India. India must realise that even the developed nations or the industrialised nations have never shut their eyes on the small and medium sector industries. These nations too appreciate the role played by SMEs in development and progress of the country.

While dealing with big foreign investors and large technology firms, India must have its SMEs in sight. The growth in India is not like pushing a cart forward, it is like pulling several strings simultaneously to keep many puppets in coordinated animation. A robust mechanism of creating 'industrial equality' is an essential ingredient of a complex economy in a country like India, where diverse factors are firmly embedded.

REFERENCES

Abhishek, Hemant. (2015) "Narendra Modi's South Korea visit: Key points of focus for India". June 2015. http://zeenews.india.com.

Ahmad, Omair. (2014). "Losing the Dragon – India-Bhutan Relations One Year after Modi's Historic Visit". October 2015. www.thehindu.com.

Anand, Shefali. (2015) "Narendra Modi's U.S. Itinerary in His Own Words". September 2015. http://blogs.wsj.com.

Aiyar, Shankar. (2015) "NextGen to GenNext...The Saga of India's Delayed Reforms. The Sunday Standard. December 19, 2015.

Arun, TK. (2015) "How to make 'Make in India'". The Economic Times. December 2, 2015.

Asano, Toshio. (2015) "Growth Through Diversity". Fortune – Asia Pacific Edition. August 1, 2015.

Bagchi, Indrani. (2015) "Modi to be first Indian PM to visit Mongolia". May 2015. http://timesofindia.indiatimes.com.

Benioff, Marc. (2015) "The 100 Best Companies To Work For". Fortune – Asia Pacific Edition. March 15, 2015.

Bhattacharya, Saurabh. (2014) "Modi-Abe's Tokyo Declaration can redefine the way world looks at Asia". September 2014. www.niticentral.com.

Burgmann, Tamsyn (2015) (The Canadian Press). "India's Modi wraps up 'successful' Canada trip". www.thestar.com.

Chand, Manish. (2015) "Act East: New Energy in India's ASEAN Journey". November 2014. www.indiawrites.org.

Chandra, Parul. (2015) "How Modi's Central Asia visit will be a game changer for India". July 2015. www.dailyo.in.

Chaudhury, Dipanjan Roy. (2015) "PM Modi's visit to Central Asia: India and Kazakhstan ink deals on uranium supply, defence". July 2015. http://economictimes.indiatimes.com.

Chaulia, Sreeram. (2015) "PM Modi's trip to Central Asia, as well as Russia, has boosted India's multi-directional strategy". July 2015. http://articles.economictimes.indiatimes.com.

Chang Mina. (2015) "Linking the World". Forbes. February 2015.

Chauhan, Chetan. (2015) "Javadekar says India happy with the Paris draft deal". Hindustan Times. December 15, 2015.

Christine. (2014) "We're Turning The Corner". Interview by Geoff Colvin in Fortune 500 – Asia Pacific Edition. June 16, 2014

Clark, Pilita and Michael Stothard. (2015) "Global warming talks hit deadlock over push to review emissions targets every five years". Financial Times. December 11, 2015.

Das, Rup Narayan. (2015) "Modi's visit to Canada is the first by an Indian PM in 42 years!" April 2015. www.rediff.com.

Ganguly, Anirban. (2014) "Why Modi's Myanmar visit signals the beginning of a realignment". November 2014. http://www.rediff.com.

Ghosh, Shubham. (2014) "Why Narendra Modi's visit to Fiji is important". November 2014. www.oneindia.com.

Ghosh, Debjani. (2015) "Brilliant Ideas are Not Enough". August, 2015. Interview by Tanmoy Goswami in Fortune India.

Goswami, Urmi. (2015) "Green pact talks hinge on finance". The Economic Times. December 7, 2015.

References

Haidar, Suhasini. (2015) "India and Mauritius announce security cooperation pact". March 2015. www.thehindu.com.

Haidar, Suhasini and Damakant Jayshi. (2014) "Many Pacts to be Signed Today (in Nepal)". November 2014. www.thehindu.com.

Heitmann, Axel C. (2014). "India Brand Equity Foundation". January 20, 2014. www.ibef.org.

India Asian News Service (IANS). (2015) "TAPI Pipeline Will Top Agenda during Indian PM Modi's Turkmenistan Visit". June 2015. www.naturalgasasia.com.

India Today. (2014) "10 highlights of Modi's visit to Japan". September 2014. http://indiatoday.intoday.in.

Indo-Asian News Service. (2014) "Modi inBangladesh: Narendra Modi praises Shiekh Hasina's Courage to Fight Terrorism". June 7, 2015. www.india.com.

Iyer, Vaidyanathan. (2014). "For Narendra Modi, first BRICS trip a success". July 2014. http://indianexpress.com.

Jagannathan, R. (2015) "Assessing the PM's US trip: Narendra Modi is the best salesman India has ever had". September 2015. www.firstpost.com.

Jopson, Barney. (2015) "Business pushes Capitol Hill hard in bid to save $700bn". Financial Times. December 9, 2015.

Juneja, Sachin. (2015) "Paving the road to global competitiveness". Mint. December 15, 2015.

Kaul, Ajay. (2014) "PM Modi's HIT plan for Nepal". August 2014. www.rediff.com.

Khan, Sadeq. (2015) "An appraisal of Modi's Dhaka visit". June 2015. www.bdchronicle.com.

Kikkoman. (2015) "A tradition of change". Fortune – Asia Pacific Edition. August 1, 2015.

Kucera, Joshua. (2015) "India's Modi Finishes Central Asia Tour in Tajikistan, Air Base Still Elusive". July 2015. www.eurasianet.org.

Lashinsky, Adam. (2014) "Apple's newest product: complexity". Fortune – Asia Pacific Edition. June 16, 2014.

Ladwig, Walter. (2015) The Telegraph, January 24, 2015.

Mackintosh, James. (2015) "Short view". Financial Times. December 9, 2015.

Maini, Tridivesh Singh. (2015) "The Significance of Modi's South Korea Visit". May 2015. http://thediplomat.com.

Mallet, Victor. (2015) "Indian reform plans thwarted again as opposition cries foul". Financial Times.December 10, 2015.

Mathews, John A. (2015) "The renewable energy revolution". Mint. December 15, 2015.

McCrum, Dan. (2015) "Short View". Financial Times. September 26, 2015.

Medhora, Shalailah. (2014) "Modi visit marks improved ties with Australia, Indian media say". November 2014. www.theguardian.com.

Merchant, Krishna. (2015) "Diversification to Asia now weighs on India's exports". Mint. December 7, 2015.

Mishra, Asit Ranjan.(2015). "New survey to quiz enterprises on effectiveness of business reforms". Mint. December 7, 2015.

Mitchell, Tom. (2015) "World bank says China risks 'getting old before getting rich'". Financial Times. December 10, 2015.

Moritz, Michael. (2015) "The fall and rise of technology juggernaut". Mint. December 4, 2015.

Murphy, R. Taggart. (2015) "Japan and the Shackles of the Past". Fortune – Asia Pacific Edition. August 1, 2015.

Murray, Alan. (2014) "The Story of Business". Fortune – Asia Pacific Edition. September 22, 2014.

Myers, Daniel P. (2014). "India Brand Equity Foundation". January 20, 2014. www.ibef.org.

Narayan, Lakshmi. (2015) "Decoding the Global Indian". Fortune India. August, 2015.

Okonjo-Iweala, Ngozi. (2014) "Leading and cleaning up Africa's largest economy". Interview by Vivienne Walt in Fortune 500 - Asia Pacific Edition. June 16, 2014.

Pant, Harsh V. (2015) "In France, Germany, and Canada, Modi Impresses". April 2015. http://thediplomat.com.

Parameswaran, Ambi MG. (2015) "Changing faces of rural market". Mint.December 15, 2015.

Patel, Aakar. (2015) "The politician you mock works harder than you". Mint. September 19, 2015.

Peri, Dinakar. (2015) "Fighter deal likely during Modi's November visit to Russia". July 2015. www.thehindu.com.

Peri, Dinakar. (2015) "In Seychelles, Modi boosts security cooperation". March 2015. www.thehindu.com.

Pillalamarri, Akhilesh. (2014) "Narendra Modi to Visit Nepal". August 2014. http://thediplomat.com.

Prakash, Smita. (2015) "Why Modi's Seychelles trip makes sense". March 2015. www.rediff.com.

Prashantham, Shameen. (2015) "China and India: Rivals and Friends?". October 2015. www.thehindu.com.

Projonmo, Notun. (2015) "Joint Declaration between Bangladesh and India during Visit of Prime Minister of India to Bangladesh". Nayi Disha. http://defence.pk.

Ramanathan, Arundhati. (2015)"Public opinion too influences business decisions". Mint. December 16, 2015.

Ranjan, Pratyush. (2015) "Modi means business: 10 highlights of PM's tour of France and Germany". April 2015. www.hindustantimes.com.

Rashid, Barrister Harun ur. (2015) "Why does Bangladesh need the Ganges Barrage?". June 2015. http://southasiamonitor.org.

Rekhi, Dia and Saloni Shukla. (2015) "We're now clearly in the midst of a recovery". The Economic Times. December 2, 2015.

Roche, Elizabeth. (2015) "What exactly did Narendra Modi's China visit yield?". November 2015. www.livemint.com.

Roche, Elizabeth. (2015) "Narendra Modi arrives in Tajikistan to cap off Central Asia visit". July 2015. www.livemint.com.

Roche, Elizabeth. (2015) "Modi wraps up Uzbek visit on week-long Central Asian tour". July 2015. www.livemint.com.

Roche, Elizabeth and Harveen Ahluwalia. (2015) "India inches up one spot in UN index". Mint. December 15, 2015.

Sahay, CD. (2015) "Prime Minister Modi's Visit to Bangladesh - A Review". June 2015. www.vifindia.org.

Sato, Yasuhiro. (2015) "Into the Big Leagues". Fortune – Asia Pacific Edition. August 1, 2015.

Saxena, Shobhan. (2015) "Prime Minister Narendra Modi kept media guessing at BRICS Summit in Brazil". July 2014. http://indiatoday.intoday.in.

Serwer, Andy. (2014). Fortune 500– Asia Pacific Edition. 16th June, 2014

Shah, Ami. (2015) "India has better growth prospects than China: Mobius". Mint. December 2, 2015.

Sharma, Rajeev. (2015) "India, Germany ink no pact, PM Modi for dedicated team to improve trade ties". April 2015. www.firstpost.com.

Sharma, Rajeev. (2015) "Forget Uranium. Real reason behind PM Modi's Mongolia visit is China". May 2015. www.firstpost.com.

Singh, Shubha. (2014) "Why Modi's visit to Fiji Islands is timely". November 2014. www.rediff.com.

Smith, Noah. (2015) "The cost of redistributing wealth". Mint. November 30, 2015.

Sood, Naresh. (2015). "PM Modi's visit to Mauritius – March 11-13, 2015". October 2015. http://citizensrightsgroup.com.

Soros, George. (2015) "Nations work best when they work together, in Europe and Beyond". Financial Times. December 17, 2015..

Stern, Nicholas. (2015) "Tough action now offers a bright future, not a hardship". Financial Times. November 27, 2015.

Sujatha. (2015) "PM Modi's Tour of Russia and Central Asia: An Overview". July 2015. www.mapsofindia.com.

Tanchum, Micha'el. (2015) "Modi and the Sino-Indian Game for Iranian Gas". July 2015. http://thediplomat.com.

The Financial Express. (2015) "Dhaka, Delhi pledge to work closely in multiple strata 'No unilateral decision' on river interlinking". June 2015. www.thefinancialexpress-bd.com.

The Independent. (2015) "River linking won't harm Bangladesh: Modi". June 2015. www.theindependentbd.com.

Thomsen, Simon. (2014) "Indian PM Narendra Modi's Australian Visit Marks A Dramatic Turnaround In Relations Between The Two Nations". November 2014. www.businessinsider.com.au.

Tourangbam, Monish and Manish Vaid. (2015) "Modi's Friendly Bhutan Visit, in a Volatile Neighborhood". http://foreignpolicy.com.

Uday India. (2015) "Modi's China Visit, Lurking Apprehension". May 2015. http://udayindia.in.

Varma, Vishnu. (2015) "Breaking down PM Narendra Modi's three-nation tour". April 2015. http://indianexpress.com.

Zee Media Bureau. (2015) "Kyrgyzstan a key part in India's Central Asia vision: PM Modi". July 2015. http://zeenews.india.com.

White, Jeff. (2014). "India Brand Equity Foundation". January 20, 2014. www.ibef.org.

Wolf, Martin (2015) "The fantasy of Britain as 'most prosperous economy'". Financial Times. November 27, 2015.

ABBREVIATIONS

AFD	Agence Française de Développement
AIF	Alternative Investment Funds
ALH	Advanced Light Helicopter
APEC	Asia-Pacific Economic Cooperation
ASEAN	Association of Southeast Asian Nations
ASSOCHAM	Associated Chambers of Commerce of India
BCIM	Bangladesh, China, India and Myanmar
BCIM-EC	Bangladesh, India, China and Myanmar Economic Corridor
BJP	Bharatiya Janta Party
BHEL	Bharat Heavy Electricals Limited
BIMSTEC	Bay of Bengal Initiative for Multi-Sectoral Technical and Economic Cooperation
BIS	Bureau of Indian Standards
BRICS	Brazil, Russia, India, China and South Africa
BSCCL	Bangladesh Submarine Cable Company Limited
BSNL	Bharat Sanchar Nigam Limited
BSTI	Bangladesh Standards and Testing Institute
BTV	Bangladesh Television

BWG	Boundary Working Group
CBIC	Chennai-Bengaluru Industrial Corridor
CBMP	Coordinated Border Management Plan
CBSL	Central Bank of Sri Lanka
CEPA	Comprehensive Economic Partnership Agreement
CEOs	Chief Executive Officers
CIS	Commonwealth of Independent States
CNC	Computerised Numerically Controlled
CoP	Conference of Parties
CSR	Corporate Social Responsibility
DFC	Dedicated Freight Corridor
DGPC	Druk Green Power Corporation
DMIC	Delhi-Mumbai Industrial Corridor
DTH	Direct to Home
EAS	East Asia Summit
EESL	Energy Efficiency Services Limited
EEU	Eurasian Economic Union
EU	European Union
EXIM	Export-Import
FDI	Foreign Direct Investment
FE	Foreign Exchange
FIP	Five Interested Parties
FIPIC	Forum for India- Pacific Islands Cooperation
FTA	Free Trade Agreement
FX	Foreign Exchange
G-20	Group of 20

Abbreviations

GAAR	General Anti Avoidance Rules
GAGAN	GPS Aided Geo Augmented Navigation system
GE	General Electric
GIAN	Global Initiative for Academic Networks
GDP	Gross Domestic Product
GST	Goods and Services Tax
GSFC	Gujarat State Fertilisers & Chemicals Ltd.
HAL	Hindustan Aeronautics Limited
ICCR	Indian Council for Cultural Relations
ICTE	International Conference on Technology and Education
IDY	International Day of Yoga
IECC	India Endowment for Climate Change
IGC	Inter-Governmental Commission
IIFCL	India Infrastructure Finance Company Limited
IIT	Indian Institute of Technology
ICWA	Indian Council of World Affairs
IED	Improvised Explosive Device
IFFCO	Indian Farmers Fertiliser Cooperative Limited
IMF	International Monetary Fund
INSTC	International North South Transport Corridor
IOR	Indian Ocean Region
IORA	Indian Ocean Rim Association
IRS	Indian Remote Sensing
IT	Information Technology
ITEC	Indian Technical and Economic Cooperation

JCM	Joint Commission on Trade, Economic, Scientific and Technical Cooperation
JWG	Joint Working Group
KASS	Korea Augmentation Satellite System
LED	Light Emitting Diode
LNG	Liquefied Natural Gas
LoC	Line of Credit
ISRO	Indian Space Research Organisation
ISIS	Islamic State in Iraq and al-Sham
JCC	Joint Consultative Commission
JRC	Joint Research Centre
MFN	Most Favoured Nation
MoU	Memorandum of Understanding
MPs	Members of Parliament
MSMEs	Micro, Small and Medium Enterprises
MSR	Maritime Silk Route
MTCR	Missile Technology Control Regime
MUDRA	Micro Units Development and Refinance Agency
NAPCI	Northeast Asia Peace and Cooperation Initiative
NASA	National Aeronautics and Space Administration
NCI	National Cancer Institute
NDRC	National Development and Reform Commission
NHPC	National Hydroelectric Power Corporation
NITI	National Institution for Transforming India

NRIs	Non-Resident Indians
NSG	Nuclear Suppliers Group
OECD	Organisation for Economic Co-operation and Development
ONGC	Oil and Natural Gas Corporation Limited
OPV	Offshore Patrol Vessel
OVL	ONGC Videsh Ltd.
PASSEX	Passing Exercise
PE	Permanent Establishment
PIC	Pacific Island Countries
PIOs	Persons of Indian Origin
PRASAD	Pilgrimage Rejuvenation and Spirituality Augmentation Drive
PCB	Printed Circuit Board
PSU	Public Sector Undertaking
PATTTTA	Pakistan, Afghanistan and Tajikistan Trilateral Transit Trade Agreement
R&D	Research and Development
RBI	Reserve Bank of India
RCEP	Regional Comprehensive Economic Partnership
REITs	Real Estate Investment Trusts
RIC	Russia, India and China
SAARC	South Asian Association for Regional Cooperation
SAR	South Asian Region
SCO	Shanghai Cooperation Organisation

SCS	South China Sea
SJVN	Satluj Jal Vidyut Nigam
SEZs	Special Economic Zones
SMEs	Small and Medium Enterprises
SNCF	French National Railways
TAPI	Tajikistan, Afghanistan, Pakistan and India
TCS	Tata Consultancy Services
UK	United Kingdom
UN	United Nations
UNCTAD	United Nations Conference on Trade and Development
UNESCO	United Nations Educational, Scientific and Cultural Organisation
UNFCCC	United Nations Framework Convention on Climate Change
UNGA	United Nations General Assembly
UNSC	United Nations Security Council
US	United States
USA	United States of America
USAID	United States Agency for International Development
WASH	Clean Water, Sanitation and Hygiene for All
WTO	World Trade Organisation